EFFECTIVE MANAGEMENT—A HUMANISTIC PERSPECTIVE

Effective Management —A Humanistic Perspective

Edited by
JOSEPH P. CANGEMI
and
GEORGE E. GUTTSCHALK

PHILOSOPHICAL LIBRARY
NEW YORK

FOR

AMELIA

AND

JUDY

Copyright, 1980, by PHILOSOPHICAL LIBRARY, INC.,
15 East 40 Street, New York, N. Y. 10016

Library of Congress Catalog Card No. 78-061106
ISBN 8022-2229-3

Manufactured in the United States of America

Foreword

It has long been my contention that it is a mistake to draw a sharp line through an organization calling one side *Management* and the other *Labor*, better known as the *We-They* concept. While it is true that some managers, by virtue of their decisions, may have a greater effect upon total organizational performance than others, it is also true that every member of an organization manages either people, machinery, money, time, or material to some extent.

The mandate for business today, as it was in the past, is profit and growth—if it is going to continue to exist. The achievement of these goals demands the mastery of techniques which old style management did not require. The make up of today's work force requires a forward plan to create and maintain a positive work environment.

It has been my good fortune to know and personally work with the authors of some of the articles included in this book. *Effective Management—A Humanistic Perspective* is designed to encourage managers and future managers to think, reflect and learn more about themselves and the environment which they help to create.

Managing is an awesome responsibility but "fun" if accomplished in a spirit of maturity and humility.

WILLIAM L. WEST,
Vice President for Manufacturing
Firestone Tire Company (U.S.)
Akron, Ohio

5

Table of Contents

Contributing Authors

JOSEPH P. CANGEMI, Ed.D., is Professor of Psychology, Western Kentucky University, Bowling Green, Kentucky.

KENNETH T. CANN, Ph.D., is Professor of Economics and Head, Department of Economics, Western Kentucky University, Bowling Green, Kentucky.

LYNN FRED CLARK, Ph.D., is Professor of Psychology and past director of the Psychology Clinic, Western Kentucky University, Bowling Green, Kentucky.

JEFFREY C. CLAYPOOL is Division Personnel Manager of the Textiles Division, Firestone Tire and Rubber Company, Gastonia, North Carolina.

CARL F. FROST, Ph.D., is Professor of Psychology at Michigan State University, in Lansing, Michigan and an international consultant in organizational development.

GEORGE E. GUTTSCHALK is Manager of Operations, Clark Equipment Corporation, Rockingham, North Carolina.

M. EUGENE HARRYMAN, Ed.D., is Professor of Education at Western Kentucky University, Bowling Green, Kentucky.

RICHARD A. HEADLEY is Corporate Manager of Education and Training at Eaton Corporation, World Headquarters, Cleveland, Ohio.

CASIMIR J. KOWALSKI, Ed.D., is Vice President, State University of New York at Morrisville, New York.

CARL R. MARTRAY, Ph.D., is Professor of Psychology, Western Kentucky University, Bowling Green, Kentucky.

DeWAYNE MITCHELL, Ph.D., is Professor of Education at Western Kentucky University, Bowling Green, Kentucky.

WILLIAM L. TAYLOR is Captain, United States Army.

This book is dedicated to the thousands of managers, from corporation presidents to front line supervisors, who have allowed us to share our ideas with them and who have demonstrated their commitment to the concept of humanistic management and leadership.

JOSEPH P. CANGEMI
GEORGE E. GUTTSCHALK

October, 1979

Editors' Preface

This book has been compiled essentially from the writings and ideas of both editors. The article by Carl Frost was selected because its content was considered complementary to the purposes of the book.

Effective Management—A Humanistic Perspective is intended to complement the ongoing activities of the editors in the areas of supervisor, management, employee and organizational development. Combined, both editors of this book have in excess of fifty years experience in teaching, training, developing, managing and leading people—both individually and in groups. Both have been associated, as either consultant or manager, with a significant number of Blue Chip, *Fortune 500* organizations and both are strongly committed to management philosophies that seek to maintain and enhance human dignity and self-regard while retaining high level productivity.

ACKNOWLEDGMENTS

Several articles contained in this book were utilized with the approval of the authors and publishers noted below:

The Carl F. Frost article was originally published as "The Scanlon Plan: Anyone for Free Enterprise?" pp. 25-33, in *MSU Business Topics*, Winter 1978. It is reprinted by permission of the Division of Research, Graduate School of Business Administration, Michigan State University.

JEFFREY C. CLAYPOOL and JOSEPH P. CANGEMI, "Complimentary Interviews: A System for Rewarding Outstanding Employees," *Personnel Journal, 57, 2,* February 1978, pp. 87-90, is reprinted by permission of *Personnel Journal.*

JOSEPH P. CANGEMI, "A Frame of Reference for Organizations," originally published as "A Frame of Reference for Organizations of Higher Education," *College Student Journal, 8, 2,* April-May 1974, pp. 67-71, is reprinted by permission of *College Student Journal.*

JOSEPH P. CANGEMI, LYNN F. CLARK and M. EUGENE HARRYMAN, "Differences between Pro-Union and Pro-Company Employees," *Personnel Journal, 55, 9,* September 1976, pp. 451-453, is reprinted with permission of *Personnel Journal.*

JOSEPH P. CANGEMI and DEWAYNE MITCHELL, "A Brief Psychology of Healthy and Unhealthy Organizations," *Psychology, 12, 2* May 1975, pp. 46-50, is reprinted by permission of *Psychology.*

13

JOSEPH P. CANGEMI, "Some Observations of American Management Personnel in Foreign Locations," originally published as "The American Overseas," *Personnel Journal, 48,* 2, pp. 118-120, February 1969, is reprinted by permission of *Personnel Journal.*

KENETH T. CANN and JOSEPH P. CANGEMI, "Peter's Principal Principle," originally published in *Personnel Journal,* Vol. 50, No. 11, pp. 872-877, November 1971, is reprinted by permission of *Personnel Journal.*

WILLIAM L. TAYLOR and JOSEPH P. CANGEMI, "Employee Theft and Organizational Climate," *Personnel Journal,* Vol. 58, No. 1, October 1979, pp. 686-689, is reprinted by permission of *Personnel Journal.*

JOSEPH P. CANGEMI and CARL R. MARTRAY, "Awareness: A Psychological Requisite for the Well Developed Personality," *Psychology, 12,* 3, August 1975, pp. 44-49, is reprinted by permission of *Psychology.*

JOSEPH P. CANGEMI, "Characteristics of Self-Actualizing Individuals," originally published as "Caracteristicas De Los Individuos Que Se Hacen A Si Mismos," *Revista De Psicologia General Y Aplicada, 31,* 138 (Journal of General and Applied Psychology), Enero-Febrero 1976, pp. 88-90, is reprinted by permission of *Revista De Psicologia General Y Aplicada,* Madrid, Spain.

SIX MISTAKES OF MAN

1. Believing that individual advancement is made by crushing others.

2. Worrying about things that cannot be changed or corrected.

3. Insisting that a thing is impossible because we cannot accomplish it.

4. Refusing to set aside preferences that are sheerly personal.

5. Neglecting the development and refinement of the mind; not acquiring the habit of reading and study.

6. Attempting to compel others to believe and live as we do.

Advanced by Cicero some 60 years before the birth of Christ.

What Employees Really Want from Their Jobs

JOSEPH P. CANGEMI *and*
GEORGE E. GUTTSCHALK

A few years back, approximately 35,000 employees were surveyed to determine what they perceived they wanted most from their jobs. The supervisors of these same employees then were surveyed to ascertain what they felt their employees wanted most from their jobs. The results of the survey are below. See Table I.

It is apparent that a wide discrepancy exists, between what supervisors perceive employees want and what employees themselves state they want from their jobs. Of particular significance are the three items ranked *highest* by employees (full appreciation for work done, feeling "in" on things, and sympathetic understanding of personal problems) and the perception of the importance of these wants on the part of supervisors. *Supervisors ranked as the three lowest wants of employees precisely what employees ranked as their three most important wants!*

The wide discrepancy in what is important on the job between the perception of employees and their managers as revealed in this survey leads to some interesting observations. Management, based on the evidence presented, erroneously believes that what

17

employees want most is material things. Even when employees and their unions demand higher wages they may be, in actuality, seeking appreciation, understanding, and a feeling of importance rather than *strictly* money. Since feeling appreciated and important is the number one need of employees, as found in this survey, and managers feel the number one need of employees is material benefits, it is apparent the paramount need of employees is not being met.

The writers, of this article have been involved with management in over 50 organizations throughout the United States and abroad and their impressions are that the need for recognition and appreciation on the part of the employees still ranks as their most frustrated need. For example, one powerful labor union with which one of the writers has worked divulged some of

TABLE I

Supervisors' Perceptions of Employees' Wants

	Employees' Ranking of What They Want	Supervisors' Ranking of What Employees Want
Full appreciation for work done	1	8
Feeling "in" on things	2	10
Sympathetic understanding of personal problems	3	9
Job security	4	2
Good wages	5	1
Interesting work	6	5
Promotion and growth with the company	7	3
Management loyalty to workers	8	6
Good working conditions	9	4
Tactful disciplining	10	7

its motivation regarding its activity against the company. Communication between this union and management had been strained for nearly two decades. When union officials finally developed some trust for the writer (after participation in one of his seminars) and had the opportunity to express themselves and indicate what they wanted from the company, 24 items were obtained from them that were important. Of the 24 items obtained, *not one* of them involved money or material benefits; 60% of them revolved around one single need: appreciation and recognition. They wanted to be shown they were important human beings in the plant. Union officials unanimously agreed that since they felt they had not been treated with respect they were forced to become the company's adversary. What they really wanted was to be treated with dignity, and if they did not get this type treatment from management they would retaliate and punish management through strong, unyielding and difficult demands for more and more material benefits and wages.

The strong suggestion coming from this research is that American industry, in general, is paying and has been paying much more, in terms of money and benefits, than perhaps it ever needed to pay. The current wages and benefits being paid to employees may have cost business and industry considerably less if managers, in particular front line supervisors, demonstrated behaviors that employees could have interpreted as "My boss cares about me." Since the data suggest employees do not feel they are appreciated as much as they would like to be, the cost to management to get its attention, quite probably, is and has been considerable.

It should be understood employees still want and enjoy material benefits. However, when the material benefits are consistently received, and will continue to be received in a predictable manner and are reasonably satisfying, the need for recognition, if not satisfied, becomes a more powerful need than the need for money, as is evidenced in this case.

The data suggest that management and labor are on a collision course. It appears management does not understand its employees. Managers *think* they do. Management appears to be imposing its values on employees. Since management's perceptions of employees' wants are inaccurate, it might be considered both groups have a high probability of developing conflict at some point in the future. See Figure I.

It is obvious the discrepancy in perception between both groups has the strong potential to lead to conflict at some point in the future. The conflict may show itself in numerous ways: wildcat strikes, strikes in general, production problems, grievances, excessive scrap, strained management-employee relations, absenteeism, tardiness, excessive tool breakage, injuries and accidents, sabotage, high turnover rate, and other behaviors that cause management to forcefully focus its attention on employees. Again, the evidence indicates the cost to management for taking its employees for granted is and has been very high indeed.

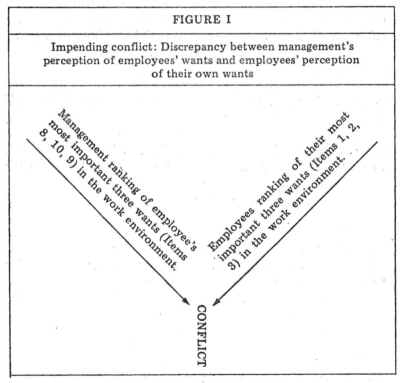

FIGURE I

Impending conflict: Discrepancy between management's perception of employees' wants and employees' perception of their own wants

CONFLICT

One of the remedies for the above situation is training for all levels of management, particularly for the front line supervisors. The authors have observed in far too numerous cases that managers, particularly front line supervisors, simply do not understand people and that the development of supervisory techniques that will help people feel important is a wise investment. The alternatives will cost much more.

Consider the case of one company of 1800 employees whose top management received consistent complaints regarding the poor relationship that existed between employees and their supervisors. As a result, the employees were attempting to establish a union to represent them. They had nearly rioted in this plant on three occasions regarding their desire to establish collective bargaining procedures for employees. With somewhere near 1100 employees eligible to vote, the voting results were as follows. On the first ballot the company won by only 15 votes. On the second ballot the company won by five votes, on the third ballot, incredibly, it was a tie. After training managers in the art of more humanistic treatment of employees, the fourth ballot found the company won by nearly 200 votes. A statistical analysis of the perception of these same employees toward their managers, several months after the termination of the training, showed a significant improvement in one area. After the training, employees rated their supervisors as having improved in demonstrating behavior which they (the employees) interpreted as "I care."

Training managers *to understand* the wants and needs of their employees obviously is good business from many perspectives.

REFERENCES

CANGEMI, JOSEPH P. A Brief Psychology of Healthy and Unhealthy Organizations. *Psychology*, Vol. 12, No. 2, May 1975, pp. 46-50.

HERSEY, PAUL and BLACHARD, KENNETH. *Management of Organizational Behavior: Utilizing Human Resources.* Englewood Cliffs, New Jersey: Prentice Hall, 1977 (Third Edition).

The Scanlon Plan–A Strategy for Organizational Development

CARL F. FROST

The Scanlon Plan had its origin in the 1930s. It concentrated on the survival needs of the economic depression and the productivity needs of the war and postwar eras. *Kiplinger* suggested the Scanlon Plan as the program to "Divvy Your Gross and Double Your Profits."[1] It was hailed by the editor of *Fortune* as "Enterprise for Everyman."[2] It has not lived up to that promise.

Joe Scanlon, the author of the concept of management and labor cooperation to assure productivity and profitability, had little anticipation or ambition of the Scanlon Plan enduring or being widely implemented. The Massachusetts Institute of Technology, through the keen foresight of Douglas McGregor, invited Scanlon to join its faculty in 1946. (The participative concept exemplified McGregor's assumption of Theory Y as contrasted to the widely exercised management assumptions of Theory X.) At the same time, McGregor invited six young instructors to introduce social science into the engineering curriculum. I was one of the instructors, and with Joe Scanlon I developed a personal and professional commitment to the Scanlon Plan as it was introduced into several New England organizations. Joe Scanlon died in 1956. Since that time M.I.T. has limited its interest in the plan to an annual conference conducted by Fred Lesieur.[3]

In 1949, as a part of Michigan State University's aggressive postwar effort to meet the needs of the ambitious returning veterans and to recognize Michigan's rapid change from an agricultural to an industrial economy, I was invited to become a member of the Department of Psychology. MSU President John A. Hannah accepted experimentally the idea of a new faculty member serving the vocationally oriented students and the changing peacetime needs for industrial productivity. President Hannah questioned whether an industrially oriented and involved faculty member could serve organizations in the state of Michigan as successfully as had the prestigious Extention Service of the College of Agriculture over many decades. I agreed to try the experiment for a year.

There were misgivings on and off the campus regarding this commitment to industrial fieldwork and consultation on the Scanlon Plan. The unions were particularly suspicious of a cooperative relationship with management in contrast to their historic adversary role. I suggested in May 1950, after a year's experience, that President Hannah have Michigan State University alumni confidentially investigate and evaluate this fieldwork. The alumni completed the assignment, at which time President Hannah endorsed the program and its continuance.

Since 1950, with the stimulation and demands of both the academic programs and the industrial organizations, the Scanlon Plan has been tested, revised, and restructured into a program for organizational development that has received increasing national and international attention. MSU has become the professional focus for the Scanlon Plan as a significant organizational development concept.

Since 1956, MSU has entered a nonprofit association of companies that have been operating their organizations under a Scanlon Plan (some companies for twenty to thirty years). This organization sponsors field studies and research on problems of executive and organizational development by master's and doctoral degree candidates.[4]

In reviewing this twenty-five-year history of Scanlon Plan experience and the research findings on organizational development, we speak with increasing confidence of what the Scanlon Plan is and is not, and for whom the Scanlon Plan process is appropriate and for whom it is not. The principles have become well documented and the process increasingly reliable.

The Scanlon Plan

The Scanlon Plan is an innovative management process for total organization development. It consists of a set of assumptions about human motivation and behavior, general principles for the management of organizations based on these assumptions, and specific procedures for implementing these principles.

Today many organizations place primary emphasis on such structural issues as who reports to whom, how best to assign people to jobs, and how to maximize efficiency through job design. Only secondary concern is given to people problems. This emphasis has created an implicitly dualistic theory in which one group—management—is the creative, directive force, totally responsible for organizational performance, and a second group—workers—exists to carry out the directives of management.

In contrast, the Scanlon Plan puts it all together. It combines the leverage of capital, the skills of managers, the creativity and competence of all employees, and the opportunities of new technology into a system supported by competent participation and equitable sharing of productivity to meet the needs of customers. In the process, an organization fulfills its proper role in the larger economic system: worthwhile employment, worthwhile goods and services, and worthwhile investments.

Experience over these years with many Scanlon Plan operations has demonstrated that an organization must focus on four critical principles:

(1) *Identity:* The extent to which employees are meaningfully informed of the organization's history, competition, customers, objectives, and so forth; identification and ownership of the current compelling need for change; and organizational development of all the employees as resources.

(2) *Participation:* The structured and guaranteed opportu-

24

nity and responsibility provided all employees to influence the decision process within the company, and to become accurately informed and responsible in their respective areas and roles of competence.

(3) *Equity:* The opportunity for all employees to realize an equitable return by increasing the investment of their resources of ideas, energy, competence, and commitment.

(4) *Managerial competence:* The inescapable necessity for management itself to establish, grow, and develop increasing professional competence and systems with assured participation from all elements of the organization's human resources.

The Scanlon Plan is not a panacea. It is not an incentive system. It is not a substitute for runaway piece-rate systems, for bitter and antagonistic industrial relations, or for incompetent executives or inadequate management systems. It is not for every organization. The Scanlon Plan is not a pat formula or set of procedures which can be mechanistically implemented with the expectation of automatically achieving a totally cooperative and productive system.

Organizational Development Prerequisites to the Scanlon Plan. The Scanlon Plan is a *process* for organizational development. The decision of whether or not to implement a Scanlon Plan requires three steps: (1) a rigorous and honest diagnosis of the organization's current level of functioning, (2) an assessment of the convincing need to change, and (3) an evaluation of the capacity to change. Inasmuch as we have detailed the principles of the Scanlon Plan elsewhere,[5] in this article I shall discuss the diagnosis, assessment, and evaluation which are critical precursors to the success of the Scanlon Plan process. These discussions present the focus of our findings in recent years.

"THE CURRENT STOCK MARKET REFLECTS THIS LACK OF CONFIDENCE IN OUR INDUSTRIAL ORGANIZATIONS' ABILITY TO GUARANTEE PREDICTABLE AND SUPERIOR RETURNS ON FURTHER INVESTMENT."

In our work with small companies and large corporations in the United States and with eight small and giant organizations in Europe, I have found the quality of leadership glaringly absent. Management is there but not leadership! A recent article by Abraham Zaleznik states the case convincingly.[6] This lack of leadership is conspicuous in the corporation and in union organizations. If we accept the definition of *leader* as that person who is perceived by followers as the best means available for getting them where they want to go at that particular time, then the dynamics of the process of exercising leadership separate the leader from the manager. Many organizations are being well managed by the accepted fiscal criteria in the short term, but they are not being led by long-term criteria which genuinely act to the advantage of the consumer-public, capital investors, or the total organization of employees.

Mandate

Your Organization As Your Investment. In the exercise of leadership, there is an initial and a singular responsibility of the leader, *vis-à-vis* the chief executive officer, to identify and define the mandate of the organization. The word *mandate* is used advisedly to state the imperatives required of the organization. These are not placed upon the company as the personal desire or prerogative of the chief executive officer, even though it is the CEO's responsibility to articulate them.

The mandate can be divided into only four or at the most five components. First is the mandate to manage the marketplace. From valid and reliable data, the chief executive officer must identify who is the customer and, just as clearly, who is not the customer. The counterpart analysis is obvious: Who is the competitor, and why does that company compete successfully? The imperative quality of that mandate comes from the customers—not the chief executive officer—who insist that they receive the best return on their investment by purchasing that organization's product and/or service. There is no long-lived brand loyalty to a product/service that does not perform, produce superior results, or pay off better than any other product. Moreover, the corollary is obvious: Without customers and more customers, there is no security or tomorrow.

Second is the mandate required to manage the physical resources of facilities, equipment, supplies, utilities, and so forth, for an imperative return on the investment. The capital expenditure has been made and will continue to be made only if the return on the investment is greater than on any alternative investment. The American public and the corporate office —not the chief executive officer—wisely and shrewdly determine their best investments. There are no real subsidies in the private, public, or government sectors for facilities that lack reliable and high levels of return. The current stock market reflects this lack of confidence in our industrial organizations' ability to guarantee predictable and superior returns on further investment.

Third is the mandate to manage with assured profitability. Profits are a cost of doing business—not a luxury or reward for a few. Both internal and external investors insist upon this level of performance and return on their committed efforts. The organization must generate capital as well as use it. This level of performance and return is demanded by the capitalist economy—not by the chief executive officer.

Fourth is the mandate to manage human resources. Again, it is not the humanity of the chief executive officer that determines this mandate. It is the action of employees who do and will insist that their employment in this organization is the best opportunity for them; otherwise, they will terminate at the earliest opportunity. It is true that some employees, including executives, paint themselves into corporate corners and haven't the courage or ability to leave. Effective management recognizes, discloses, and declares the mandate of the employees at all levels that this company affords them the best employment opportunity and responsibility. In the economic vernacular, employment here offers them the best personal and professional returns on their investments of energy, education, training, expertise, life.

Fifth is the mandate, not present in every organization, to develop and manage the unique technology required to survive and succeed. The technology is not the fancy of the owner or chief executive officer, but is required to meet the special needs of the customers, investors, and employees if they are going to consider this organization first. The mandate might be expressed by an organization as the imperative to be number one in electronic technology or the best in short-term intensive health care, and so forth.

The clear compelling identification of the mandate in these five areas, documented by the valid and reliable data showing that their fulfillment is imperative, is the initial responsibility of the chief executive officer. To date I have not encountered one organization that has fulfilled this need and expectancy of the organization for its own mandate. We have been shown mission statements, goals, objectives, annual and long-term plans—but not the mandate. We have been shown lengthy platitudinous rhetoric—but no simple and succinct (one-page) statement of the convincing imperatives of the marketplace, the capital investors, and the employees.

A particular feature of the mandate is that the chief executive officer does not get involved or include the means of achieving the mandate. This is the responsibility of the immediate staff and succeeding levels of management, in increasing detail and specificity. If chief executive officers are meeting their appropriate responsibilities, they are less competent in the technical implementation and professional expertise of each mandated area. They must be confident and prove to their organizations that there is the competence in their organizations to achieve the mandate as required in each area.

Finding Out about Your Company as Your Investment. Once the mandate is identified, then executive staff members, as a group, are informed and requested to challenge, clarify, and vouch for the validity and reliability of the data supporting the respective mandates of marketing, physical resources, profit, human resources, and technology. If chief executive officers present mandates as their personal edicts rather than as working papers, they will serve neither themselves nor their organizations. In a large corporation, the mandate for any division or operation is completely consistent with the corporate expectancies of the management of these areas. Often, the full disclosure of the corporate expectancies or the chief executive officer's statement with supporting data is surprising to many members of the staff. There is generally wide variability of the awareness and acceptance of the mandate. To *understand* the mandate—not merely to know it—may require several hours and occasions of intensive discussion to avoid polite or traditional acceptance and conformance. To process the mandate appropriately is a supreme test of leadership.

"ON SEVERAL OCCASIONS THE CHIEF EXECUTIVE OFFICER AND/OR STAFF HAVE DECIDED THAT THEY WERE NOT READY TO PROCEED. THOSE DECISIONS HAVE PROVED TO BE WISE."

When the executive staff group appears ready, the chief executive officer requests a secret vote on the question: "Do you understand the mandate?" Almost all staff members demur and claim their staffs do not need to vote secretly. "We are frank, open, and ready to declare our position." That is a cop-out. After such an intensive and frank discussion and challenge of the mandate, the integrity of the chief executive officer and of each staff member deserves and demands a secret vote. If there are abstentions or negative votes, it means more data and study are required to support the questioned areas. It remains the responsibility of the chief executive officer to rework and resubmit the data and revised mandate. When the staff members *understand* the mandate and its implications, and a positive vote is secretly and responsibly made, the staff proceeds to the second question.

The second question is a personal confrontation. "Are you able and willing to accept the ownership of the problem?" If the staff members understand the mandate and its implications for them, this is a new question. For example, when a particular corporation set a mandate that doubled the gross profit required with no new product introductions for five years, the controller resigned, or rather took early retirement. In another situation, when a hospital board of directors froze the operating costs for two years, the administrator resigned. There should be genuine soul searching and review of other personal alternatives before the secret vote is taken. The chief executive officer and staff members need to know the result of this vote, too. If it is satisfactory, then the third question is appropriate.

This question concerns the ability and willingness to make a commitment to achieving the mandate. It has three parts. The first is a challenge to each individual: "Are you personally competent to fulfill your assignment under the mandate?" The inquiry obviously challenges all staff members to decide if this *is* their best job opportunity. The second part is a challenge to the members of the executive group: "Is there the required competence represented in each other executive member to accomplish the mandate?" Staff members would be foolhardy to join a team which was not competently and completely staffed to achieve the mandate. The third part requires all staff members to declare specifically what they will do—differently— to assure the fulfillment of the mandate. This declaration is not more of the same but the recognition of a needed change in quality and quantity of personal and professional investment in their assignments. This third part takes place at a specifically set meeting with adequate time for preparation. During discussion of the third part, it becomes obvious to the chief executive officer and all staff members whether each one understands the mandate, is able and willing to accept the ownership of the problem, and has the competence and commitment to fulfill this responsibility. Only after this rigorous confrontation, a third secret vote is appropriately requested by the chief executive officer: "Are you able and willing to make a commitment to the achievement of the mandate?"

Each vote must be prefaced by the admonition that all members now have all the data and therefore should vote responsibly for themselves, their colleagues, and the organization. On several occasions the chief executive officer and/or staff have decided that they were not ready to proceed. Those decisions have proved to be wise. Obviously, under these conditions the preparatory steps toward the formal Scanlon Plan consideration are held in abeyance. In the meantime the organization usually proceeds to develop itself toward readiness to make a commitment.

This mandate process is most challenging. It establishes the bases, principles and operating rules, and disciplined relationships at the top echelon. Unless and until the process is completed satisfactorily with the executive staff, the process is not pursued at lower echelons.

What to Do about Your Investment in the Company. I will describe the process of judging one's investment in the company by outlining a recent case, exploring the appropriateness of the Scanlon Plan for a particular organization.

The Customer Investor: The processing of the mandate was completed throughout this 1,600-person organization, beginning with the executive staff, then the operating staff, then the supervisors, and then the operating personnel. The mandate was specifically and operationally documented and illustrated for each department.

The product is a widely used consumer product, visible in the marketplace. Consequently, in discussing the market mandate the question was asked of all personnel: "How many of you use our own product?" The response was far less than 50 percent. They were challenged by the conclusion that personally they did not believe their product was their best investment. Why? Was the problem quality? Service? Price?

Obviously, competitors were enjoying their patronage and loyalty. The inroads of this conspicuous competition were documented and quickly recognized as a genuine threat to the employee's own job security.

The Capital Investor: The facts were revealed as to the conspicuous and substantial investment the corporation had made in this facility and equipment and, consequently, the imperative need to operate it continuously and far more profitably.

The economic data on the required return on investment were disclosed, as was the identity of the capital investors. The American public had had confidence in the corporation stock which had made this new facility and technology possible. Would the stock market investors continue to have this confidence?

31

The alternatives that capital investors can exercise were identified. The less-than-adequate profit position of the industry was discussed candidly and constructively. Applications were made to the corporation and to this specific operation.

The Employee Investor: The employees were asked about their satisfaction with their jobs. There was almost unanimous agreement that their jobs now were the most desirable, best paying, and most promising in the community.

When challenged about their need for more and additional benefits next year, there was complete agreement on expectations. When they were asked how to assure the continuing ability of the corporation to meet these needs, there was less agreement. It was objectively documented that unless significant improvements in efficiencies resulted in greater profitability, there would be insufficient funds in the bank upon which to draw increased checks for salaries and benefits.

In summary, the organization personnel were informed, educated, and then challenged with three primary responsibilities:

(1) that all customers should be convinced that they receive the best return on their investment by purchasing this company's product and services;

(2) that American citizens who invest in the stock market and corporate officers all should be convinced that they receive the highest return on their investments in the form of money and of production schedules for this division;

(3) that all employees should be convinced that they receive the best return on their job investment of time, energy, knowhow, education, and suggestions by employment in this company.

Once this education process was completed in small groups, a secret vote was taken on four questions:

Are you convinced that there is a compelling need to change?
Is there a genuine potential for improvement?
What is in it for you?
Do you want to participate in developing a proposal (Scanlon Plan) through an elected Ad Hoc Committee to achieve this change?

There were 35 negative votes among more than 1,600 employees in an organization that was already the best operation in the corporation. The employees *understood* the mandate. They were able and willing to *accept the problem ownership*. They were *committed* to achieving the mandate of the customers, investors, and employees.

The fulfillment of the fourth question was the election of the Ad Hoc Committee. Each department and shift had a representative. The 75 members were divided into three committees of 25. The Education Committee had the responsibility for documenting the need to change and the reasons the Scanlon Plan was appropriate. The Rules and Regulations Committee had the assignment of handling the elections, terms of office, functions of the Production and Screening Committee that would be formed, and procedures for handling suggestions. The Formula Committee had the assignment of developing the bases and formula for calculating a monthly bonus in such a way that all employees would recognize their accountability under the Scanlon Plan.

This process assured the coauthorship of the Scanlon Plan. The Ad Hoc Committee's work was made final in notebook form. Every company should write its own book. An addendum was prepared from all the questions asked during the inquiries. It appeared in the form of "a quiz you cannot fail" with true and false answers and explanations. This quiz ensured that the majority of employees were confronted with the possible issues, concerns, and questions that might arise in their new experience under the Scanlon Plan. There would be few surprises. The final page of the book was a sample ballot for the secret vote. Of course, the preface included the signatures of all Ad Hoc Committee authors.

The Rules and Regulations Committee had established the majority vote required to introduce the plan. It is usual to require a 90 percent majority to document the level of commitment required to assure success.

As the reader can readily comprehend, this process is a demanding organizational education. It assures that the majority of the employees know the organizational realities of the marketplace, the required return on investment of physical resources, the cost of profits, and the appropriate use of human resources. It also declares (in actual percentages) that the employees are or are not able and willing to accept the ownership of the problem and become responsible. Every step is essential. One client decided it could not afford to educate all its people —only 400 out of 900 employees. The vote failed to meet the required 90 percent majority. Another client did not work patiently and closely enough with the union local. The local union officers were not able and/or willing to accept the ownership of the problem. Consequently, when the vote was taken, the union members followed the entrenched leadership of their local president, as was predictable from a militant history, and an insufficient majority was returned. The process does require time, patience, and sequential steps to build confidence in one another and trust in the operational facts.

Scanlon Plan Principles Over Twenty-five Years

Doing the Right Job and Doing the Job Right. The mandate and its process assure the chief executive officer and all of the employees of "doing the *right job*" (Peter Drucker's definition of effectiveness). The authorship through the Ad Hoc Committee and implementation of the Scanlon Plan through the Production and Screening committees assure the chief executive officer and the employees of "doing the *job right*" (Drucker's definition of efficiency).

"EMPLOYEES EXPECT AND RESPECT THIS DISCIPLINE FROM RATIONAL MANAGEMENT."

The process of doing the right job and doing the job right continues during operations under the Scanlon Plan. The mandate, rules and regulations, and formula are continually reviewed for validity and reliability. Changes are infrequent, but life is change and consequently should be managed by everyone. The changing operational reality of the organization requires periodic review and revision of the Scanlon Plan to serve everyone's best interest and equity.

The leadership of an organization that has been implementing the Scanlon Plan for many years follows the basic principles outlined in the book referred to earlier. In the first principle, *identity*, the chief executive officer and staff members recognize the organization's continual historical successes and failures. They must keep the entire organization alert to the need to change in order to manage the marketplace, physical resources, profitability, and human resources. In this process the customers, the investors, and employees have increasing confidence that they get the best return on their investments and that management is serving them well. The company must continually be alert and develop its unique reason for being or it will lose its identity and commitment. Under a Scanlon Plan, management has an additional demand—identification and development of all employees as important resources who are accountable from their first day of indoctrination to the end of their careers.

In their second principle, *participation*, the long-term Scanlon Plan company must be sensitive to the increasing employee demand for more accurate and timely information as well as more prompt response to their questions and suggestions. Employees become more able and willing to participate and accept genuine responsibility when the rationality of management's decisions is obvious. When the rationality of the employee's questions, challenges, and suggestions is accepted and acted upon by management, the employees' trust and commitment increase. The process is never permissive. Management, whether it is the supervisor in the Production Committee or the executive in the Screening Committeee, must exercise genuine leadership in decision making. When certain organizations experimented recently by delegating the work situation to the employees and reducing supervision, the employees found the situation confusing, unwanted, and unsatisfactory. There is a discipline which the reality of customers, capital investors, and employees demands. Employees expect and respect this discipline from rational management.

The third principle that is always worth guarding and assuring is *equity*. The quality of equity must be assured among all the parties—customers, investors, and employees. When quantitative records of production are made at the expense of safety, quality, or customer service, there is no reason to celebrate with a bonus. Equity is often in the eye of the beholder, so it is essential to assess continuously the perception of all the organization's members—customers, investors, and employees. Are they convinced of equitable return on their investment in the company?

When the Scanlon Plan really becomes established and the organization matures, there is an awesome demand for *competence of management and management systems,* the fourth Scanlon Plan principle. The epitome of this maturity occurs when all employees of staff and line come to their daily assignments with the assurance that every aspect of their jobs is rational. That quality demands the greatest ability up front to manage the marketplace, physical resources, profitability and human resources. After twenty-five years of experience, Scanlon Plan management is still striving to achieve this level of effectiveness and efficiency, so every employee considers every management decision rational.

Today, whether the Scanlon Plan is established in a hospital, school, industrial firm, or government agency, its success as an organizational development process must assure that the marketplace (the patient, student, consumer, or public), the capital investors, and the employees realize their best returns by investing in that product and/or service.

The process must identify among all employees the comprehension of the problem (mandate) and the overt (secretly voted—90 percent majority) ability and willingness to accept the ownership of the problem.

The process must identify the ruthless need for competence of all personnel who do make a commitment to achievement of the corporate mandate.

Socialistic Systems Versus Capitalist Economies

The free enterprise or capitalist system uniquely affords management this opportunity and responsibility for organizational development. In recent work with organizations in the European socialistic systems (Strømmen Steel, Volvo, British Steel, I.C.I., and others), I found that this opportunity is no longer available. Management and the unions, for example, turned over to the British government the responsibility for the steel industry ten years ago, abdicating their problem-ownership responsibility.

At Volvo, it seems that innovative programs directed toward the quality of working life fail to assure the competitive competence to survive in world markets.[7] The cost of labour in Sweden is the highest in the world, and the employees cannot tell whether Volvo or their government is the benefactor sustaining high employment in a diminishing marketplace. Is it rational to fail to disclose the facts of life? Is it humane not to give people the right and responsibility to earn their survival, security, and success? In the long run, the reality of the competitive marketplace—and not management—is going to decide.

I.C.I. has developed and carried out innovative approaches to organizational development to gain increased productivity and profitability. The ingenuity and superlative effort have been magnificent, as documented by Joe Roeber.[8] The effort is generally recognized as having tragically failed to gain the unions' acceptance of the ownership of the problem. The unions did participate in the procedures. That is not the same process as ownership of the problem and then commitment to its resolution. The sequence of ownership-of-the-problem to resolution-of-the-problem is essential in any human or organizational relationship.

"THE SCANLON PLAN PROCESS CHALLENGES BOTH THE LEADERSHIP AND MANAGERSHIP OF ALL INDUSTRIAL AND SERVICE ORGANIZATIONS."

The socialist countries have conspicuously lost interest in productivity in favor of employee participation. This participation is epitomized by legislated membership on the boards of directors. The Bullock Report defines such matters as size of organizations that are required to establish joint boards, number of constituents on the boards, eligibility of certain union members and officials, as well as boardroom protocol.[9] However, these boards of directors participate in business as usual rather than considering critical issues and problems of survival, productivity, competitive positions, and profitability. It seems these boards have not developed the leadership which defines and articulates the mandate of the worldwide marketplace, of the required return on investment of any and all physical resources, and of the employees' needs and expectances of more than a minimum wage. These boards delegated their future comfort and security to the government long ago. This is another case of inability or unwillingness to accept the problem ownership.

Leaving the foreign socialist systems and evaluating our two hundred years of free enterprise we might ask: Is there leadership—or just managership—in American industry and unions today? The criteria of growth and profitability of auto manufacturers suggest conspicuous managership. But escalating costs, sharply rising foreign car sales, and resistance to solving energy resource constraints question the quality of leadership. The reference could be made to many industries and agencies in the United States.

The Scanlon Plan process challenges both the leadership and managership of all industrial and service organiations. It is not the only system. It is not for every organization; in fact, relatively few are able or willing to accept its premises or meet its demands. It requires that every member of the organization, beginning with the chief executive officer, serve the committed investors: the customers, the investors, and the employees. Otherwise, our egos, like that of a recent U.S. president, blind us to our own constituents' needs, and consequently we fail to release that infinite potential of heterogenity, genius, effort, and commitment for the good of all.

How long will our free enterprise system support our "life, liberty, and pursuit of happiness" in a realistic, caring and sharing world that is honest enough, proud enough, creative enough to accept opportunity and responsibility, and not subsidy?

REFERENCES

1. "Divvy Your Gross and Double Your Profits." *Kiplinger Magazine,* 2 (December 1948):31-3.
2. DAVENPORT, RUSSELL W. "Enterprise for Everyman." *Fortune,* 41 (January 1950):55-9, 152, 157-59.
3. LESIEUR, FRED, ed. *The Scanlon Plan: A Frontier in Labor Management Cooperation.* Cambridge, Mass.: M.I.T. Press, 1958.
4. RUH, ROBERT A., WHITE, J. KENNETH, GREENWOOD, WILLIAM, III, HILL, THOMAS, LOWMAN, RODNEY, and MESSICCI, JOSEPH are doctoral graduates who have been involved in this work.
5. FROST, C. F., WAKELY, J. H., and RUH, R. A. *The Scanlon Plan for Organization Development: Identity, Participation, and Equity.* East Lansing: MSU Press, 1974.
6. ZALEZNIK, ABRAHAM. "Managers and Leaders: Are They Different?" *Harvard Business Review,* 55 (May-June 1977):67-78.
7. AGUREN, STEFAN, HANSSON, REINE, and KARLSSON, K. G. "The Volvo Kalmar Plant: The Impact of New Design on Work Organization." September 1976, The Rationalization Council, SAF LO.
8. ROEBER, JOE. "Social Change at Work: The I.C.I. Weekly Staff Agreement." London: Gerald Duckworth and Company Limited, 1975.
9. CHAIRMAN LORD BULLOCK. "Report of the Committee of Inquiry on Industrial Democracy." Department of Trade. London: Her Majesty's Stationery Office, 1977.

Complimentary Interviews: A System for Rewarding Outstanding Employees

JEFFREY C. CLAYPOOL *and*
JOSEPH P. CANGEMI

Rating employees is a continuous, day-to-day process which occurs in a work environment where supervisors and managers are responsible for the performance of subordinates. Management at all levels must constantly evaluate the performance of employees, whether formally or informally.

In today's work setting, where documentation is so important, training programs often are directed towards report writing and corrective action. However, in the fast-changing industrial world, the tendency is to forget to document the foundation of every successful business: the dedicated, dependable and hard-working employees. Consider that employees spend approximately 25% of their time each year in a work environment, however pleasant or unpleasant it might be. The survival of every organization depends upon these individuals, and management should feel as strongly about documenting their outstanding skill and reliability as it does in censoring those employees who are careless about attendance, safety, quality, cost and production. This forgetfulness is not often intentional, but it eventually accentuates the negative rather than the positive aspects of employee performance. In dwelling on the negative, managers and supervisors ignore many of the concepts that contribute toward job satisfaction.

It is also reasonable to conclude that any long-lived and successful business has had more good performance from its employees than poor. Management needs to do more to avoid a frequent complaint among workers: "The only time my supervisor talks with me about performance is when I do something wrong." Management at all levels should spend more time complimenting the abilities and successes of employees and trying to establish a climate of respect, concern, trust and appreciation. As a means of doing so, managers might consider taking the initiative to institute a plantwide system of complimentary interviews for those employees who merit such consideration.

Theories of Motivation

Research indicates that reasons for job satisfaction include such items as achievement, recognition, responsibility, growth and other factors associated with the motivation of the individual on the job.[1,2,4,6,7]

Industrial psychologists have spent considerable time studying and discussing motivation and different types of individual needs. The motivational theories developed by Maslow, Herzberg and McGregor have received particular attention during recent years. Maslow's widely discussed Need Hierarchy[5] relates human needs and individual behavior. He suggested that an individual's needs may be ranked into five categories, from the strongest to the least demanding:

- *Physiological,* or basic needs, such as oxygen, water, sleep and food

- *Safety,* or the need of a stable environment relatively free of threats (e.g., loss of employment)

- *Acceptance,* or the need to be recognized and accepted as a group member by one's peers

41

■ *Esteem,* or the need for self-respect, self-esteem, the esteem of others, recognition, prestige and praise

■ *Self-actualization,* or the need for self-fulfillment, personal growth and development, and worthwhile accomplishments.

Maslow also pointed out various management principles and assumptions that underlie conditions necessary for a healthy organizational environment.[4] Consider the assumptions listed below:

1. In each employee there is a need to achieve.
2. Each employee prefers to feel important, useful, successful, proud of accomplishments and respected by fellow employees.
3. Each employee likes to be appreciated, especially in public. Employees like to talk about their accomplishments and likewise enjoy hearing others praise them. The praise, however, must be realistic and fair. If employees are praised for work that is not performed according to established standards, this can actually produce guilt feelings or other problems.

A study by Herzberg, Mausner and Synderman[3] evaluated the causes of job satisfaction and dissatisfaction of engineers and accountants and has been subject to considerable attention, praise and criticism. Results found that certain job factors associated with high satisfaction or *satisfiers* were somewhat different from other job aspects that were associated with low satisfaction or *dissatisfiers.* They found that the satisfiers included achievement, recognition, advancement, responsibility and praise. Dissatisfiers seemed to center around policy, supervision, salary, working conditions, etc. Apparently satisfiers (or motivators) lead to job satisfaction and dissatisfiers lead to dissatisfaction.

Douglas McGregor in his book *The Human Side of Enterprise*[6] encouraged managers and supervisors to review and analyze their own beliefs about managerial styles in hope they would test them against reality, read surveys and other research, and mold this knowledge into a management strategy of accomplishment. McGregor emphasized that physical and mental effort in work is as natural as recreation or rest and that employees will exercise self-direction and self-control in the attainment of objectives to which they are committed. He also emphasized that employees will not only accept responsibility, but will even seek it out, especially if their commitment to accomplish objectives is a result of rewards associated with the achievement of the same objectives. Recognition and praise are considered meaningful rewards by employees and are strongly desired and sought by them. It is, of course, noteworthy that Maslow, Herzberg and McGregor each perceive achievement, praise and recognition as playing an important part in the theory of job satisfaction.

Both theory and experience lead the authors to a consistent observation: Recognition is the most frustrated need of employees, especially factory employees. But satisfying this need for appreciation does not seem to be a high management priority when one reviews the spectrum of company-sponsored and initiated activities and programs for industrial employees. The concept of showing appreciation in other than economic and recreational form is apparently all too often neglected.

The Complimentary Interview

The general purpose of a complimentary interview is to positively evaluate personnel and to give them performance feedback, recognition and praise, to highlight potential, and to enhance organizational planning. More specifically, the following purposes are served by such an interview:

- *Employee Promotion*—The identification of employees who are eligible for promotion with the discussion of each employee's strengths.

- *Employee Transfer*—The identification of employees who have the necessary abilities to transfer laterally to another job, whether it be in another department, plant or division of the company. Again, attention is given to the employee's strengths.

- *Performance Feedback*—Nearly all employees seek performance feedback with respect to their jobs, regardless of the responsibilities. Emphasis again must be on strengths.

■ *Employee Improvements*—Analysis is made of an employee's strong points so that both management and the employee can direct their efforts toward the development of personal characteristics, skills and abilities that will increase the worker's chances of promotion. Employees want and need guidance on how to continually improve their performance.

■ *Employee Training*—The identification of training and development plans to further assist the employee in maximizing effort and performance. Strengths and development of the strengths are always emphasized.

■ *Need Satisfaction*—Satisfaction of employee needs in the areas of safety, esteem, self-fulfillment and self-actualization. Employees who receive recognition for their strengths develop confidence in themselves and respect for the company that contributed to this confidence.

■ *Improved Morale*—The improvement of employee morale through stimulating confidence in management's fairness and concern for the employees' emotional needs. The manager/supervisor and the employee can develop a good personal relationship whereby each has a better understanding of the other, and the employee is made to feel needed as an individual, not just a number or a tool. The employee whose strengths have been observed and appreciated generally becomes a more confident and hard-working member of the organization.

In all human beings there is a strong desire to be approved and respected by others. Employees want to know how their work is regarded by their managers or supervisors, especially when the manager or supervisor will have some say about promotional opportunities. Informing people of their job status naturally has a strong bearing on their feelings of safety and security. Complimentary interviews can both assist management in advising employees of their outstanding performance and increase their feelings of job security and loyalty to the company. Conversely, feelings of insecurity and disloyalty within an employee are aggravated by lack of information about the employee's status.

The complimentary interview program should involve several individuals: the employee, supervisor, the plant manager, the department manager, the personnel manager and the employee's family. The employee and the supervisor are generally the only participants in the actual interview. The supervisor must find a private place where they can talk and be free from distraction. First, the supervisor should explain the purpose of the complimentary interview and the importance of this program to the employee and the company. It should be made clear to the employee that complimentary interview reports are given to commend employees for superior performance. The manager or supervisor must use sound judgment as to how often or when to hold a complimentary interview, as it becomes meaningless if given too often, on an erratic basis, or for average performance. Consistency is very important and the supervisor should develop standards to be used as guidelines that will enhance the interview's values. These standards may vary according to a supervisor's personal philosophy, the work environment, and the

---

CONSISTENT STANDARDS OF RECOGNITION ARE
ONE THING, BUT FAVORITISM IS ANOTHER.

---

degree to which good performances have previously been recognized in a particular area of work. For example, if assemblers are not used to hearing their efforts praised, then the supervisor might initially set somewhat lower performance standards for them. Otherwise, the most important aspect of the program is that all qualified employees receive complimentary interviews for the same level of performance. Unless employees are convinced that there is no favoritism involved, the value of complimentary interviews will be reduced substantially.

The first complimentary interview will give the manager or supervisor the opportunity to discuss how the employee feels about his/her job performance, career progress and promotability. The employee also might be asked what type of help is needed in order to be more successful. The employee even might be interested in helping to establish higher standards or objectives that would trigger additional interviews. Often employees who are consulted about their work will set more difficult goals for themselves than those established by a manager or supervisor, and they will find meeting these goals an interesting challenge in an otherwise routine job. The aim of this approach is not to enrich employees' jobs, but rather to create a more responsive and satisfying work climate.

Unfortunately, there are some supervisors who automatically assume that their subordinates are untrustworthy, lazy and incapable of the initiative necessary to establish job objectives. However, when employees are accorded the same respect and attention that managers or supervisors want themselves, the re-

---

THE AIM: TO CREATE A SATISFYING
WORK CLIMATE.

---

sults can benefit all concerned. Many employees would like a more challenging job and more appreciation from management might motivate them to contribute innovative ideas. Conversely, there are other workers who do not want greater job challenge, but who do want their efforts respected, recognized and praised.

A brief summary of the employee's performance should also be written, stating that the success of the company and the employee is due to his or her outstanding performance in any one of several areas. This statement should be signed by the manager or supervisor, be completely reviewed with the employee, and then signed by the latter as well. The employee should also know that copies of the written summary will be sent to the department manager or foreman, the personnel and factory managers, and the employee's home for future reference and rereading. All of this, of course, is designed to further bolster the worker's self-esteem.

The department manager, the personnel manager and the plant manager should make it a point to visit the employee at his/her work location and offer congratulations for receiving the complimentary interview, and reiterate why outstanding performance is appreciated by the company and needed in a successful plant operation. It is important to recognize that the work station is just as important to the employee as an office is to a manager or supervisor. A special trip into the plant to congratulate the employee helps to destroy territorial barriers. A

A SPECIAL TRIP INTO THE PLANT TO
CONGRATULATE AN EMPLOYEE
HELPS BREAK DOWN
TERRITORIAL BOUNDARIES.

---

company newspaper can also highlight good performance, but any suspicion of favoritism must be avoided.

Reinforcing the Program

Will managers and supervisors have time to carry out the program?

One neglected consideration in setting up a complimentary interview program is the demands the system makes on a supervisor's time. It is all well and good for management to state that nothing is more important than periodically praising and recognizing outstanding performance, but the fact remains that complimentary interviews are in competition with other responsibilities. The manager or supervisor also may feel the accomplishment of these other responsibilities has a more direct bearing on his/her own achievements and promotions. This presents a problem because an adequate complimentary interview program requires managers or supervisors to devote much time to discussion, writing, and setting standards, if the results are to be worthwhile. Many managers or supervisors either are unwilling to give the required time or just do not care enough about such a program to develop it.

There are several ways in which this problem can be approached:

1. Top management should take an active interest in the complimentary interview program and give it strong sup-

port. Top management should also develop a complimentary interview program for staff and department level managers. This will go a long way toward ensuring that complimentary interviews are given a good chance for success in the competition for the manager's or supervisor's time and allow the program to filter downward through the organization.

2. Higher-level management should encourage the distribution of the complimentary interview forms so that the managers or supervisors complete a few each month.

3. Top management should guide and assist the managers/supervisors in setting objectives with respect to the standards and quantity of complimentary interviews.

Developing the Complimentary Interview Form

The development of the complimentary interview *statement* is relatively simple. Listed at the top of the page is information about the employee and the manager or supervisor, such as name, credited service date, department, job classification, shift, manager's or supervisor's name, length of time under his/her supervision and the subject to be discussed. An adequate amount of space then should be left for the supervisor or manager to write a brief summary of the outstanding performance. There should be a signature line at the bottom of the page for the manager or supervisor *and* employee to sign. Copies should be marked as forwarded to the factory manager, department manager, personnel manager or other designated officials.

The complimentary interview program allows management to share respect, praise, concern, trust and appreciation with employees in a formal way. There is evidence that this sort of management/employee communication tends to produce a strong, committed and efficient work force. This approach does not require direct financial investment on the part of the company—only time. On the contrary, even the smallest decrease in waste, cost or absenteeism, or an increase in safety, production, and quality, is a good return on the investment of complimentary interviews.

REFERENCES

1. CANGEMI, JOSEPH and MITCHELL, DEWAYNE. A Brief Psychology of Healthy and Unhealthy Organizations. *Psychology*, Vol. 12, No. 2, 1975, pp. 46-50.
2. LIKERT, RENSIS. *New Patterns of Management*. New York: McGraw-Hill Book Co., Inc., 1961.
3. LUTHANS, FRED. *Organizational Behavior*. New York: McGraw-Hill Book Co., Inc., 1973.
4. MASLOW, ABRAHAM. *Eupsychian Management*. Homewood, Illinois: Richard D. Irwin, Inc. and The Dorsey Press, 1965.
5. MASLOW, ABRAHAM. *Motivation and Personality*. New York: McGraw-Hill Book Co., Inc., 1970.
6. McGREGOR, DOUGLAS. *The Human Side of Enterprise*. New York: McGraw-Hill Book Co., Inc., 1960.
7. McGREGOR, DOUGLAS. *The Professional Manager*. New York: McGraw-Hill Book Co., Inc., 1967.

A Frame of Reference for Organizations

JOSEPH P. CANGEMI *and*
CASIMIR J. KOWALSKI

All organizations have goals, and these goals are achieved through individuals. Some organizations are highly effective in the pursuit and attainment of their goals; others achieve only a small portion of them, and often with great difficulty. One of the significant underlying factors associated with organizational success is the attitude held toward people. An organization's philosophy about people in general will have much influence on the attainment of its goals. This philosophy will determine much policy and will play a significant role in morale. Whether an organization appreciates it or not, its philosophy toward man will either enhance its opportunities for success or decrease them significantly.

Organizations are developed because they provide man with the vehicle to accomplish goals he could not accomplish alone.

Organizing human effort is a problem and has always been a problem. The Mayan chief building a temple faced problems and difficulties similar to those faced by a university president or corporation president. Each has to determine (1) how to organize work; (2) how to allocate workers; (3) how to recruit, train and effectively manage the individuals available to do the work; (4) how to create work conditions and reward and punishment systems which will enable the employees to maintain high effectiveness and adequate morale over long periods of time; (5) how to adjust their organizations to change and technological innovations; and (6) how to cope with competition or harassment from sub-groups within their own organizations (Schein, 1970). Obviously, these problems of organizations have not changed much over the centuries.

What Is An Organization?

According to Schein (1970), an acceptable definition of an organization is

> ... the rational coordination of the activities of a number of people for the achievement of some common explicit purpose or goal, through division of labor and function, and through a hierarchy of authority and responsibility.

Before one can accomplish organizational goals, one must first establish an underlying philosophy upon which the organization will rest. This philosophy has to do with *man,* since organizations are essentially groups of men. A philosophy of the nature of man must be at the base of any organization; indeed, it is its very foundation. Table I shows that a philosophy of man is the founding stone upon which the rest of the organization is built, behaviorally speaking. The underlying assumptions about man determine how an organization treats its employees, professional or otherwise. They will determine in what manner organizational goals will be achieved.

An interesting classification of organizations was done by Etzioni (1964), based on the type of authority system utilized by them. This classification and comparison of the organizations is insightful. See Table II. Organizations that control through coercive power tend to have members who would not belong and who are alienated but who are coerced to remain. Utilitarian oriented organizations tend to have members who are calculating

51

TABLE I

The Place of a Philosophy of Man in Organizations

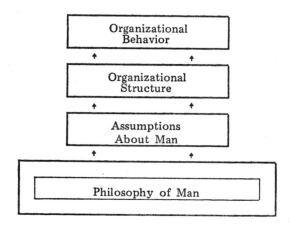

and who anticipate material rewards for their performance but do not necessarily feel positive toward their superiors, their employer or their jobs. Organizations that base their authority on a normative philosophy tend to have members who belong because they identify with the goals of the organization and feel some moral commitment to the organization and the role they play in it.

The Nature of Man: Four Assumptions

Historically, there have been four basic assumptions about the nature of man. They evolved chronologically in the order presented: 1) Rational-economic man; 2) social-man; 3) self-actualizing man; 4) complex-man (Schein, 1970).

Rational-economic man as a philosophy sees man as essentially hedonistic; selfish, calculating, cunning, scheming, maximizing his selfish interests and behaving accordingly. Man behaves in ways that produce the greatest economic gain. He will permit himself to be manipulated in order to obtain economic and materialistic goals. Man essentially is irrational and must be harnessed lest his feelings get out of control and he damages himself

TABLE II

Classifications of Organizations Based on
Type of Power or Authority Used

Predominantly coercive authority
  Concentration Camps
  Prisons and correctional institutions
  Prisoner-of-war camps
  Custodial mental hospitals
  Coercive unions

Predominantly utilitarian rational-legal authority, use of economic
rewards
  Business and industry (with a few exceptions)
  Business unions
  Farmers organizations
  Peacetime military organizations

Predominantly normative authority, use of membership, status,
intrinsic value rewards
  Religious organizations (churches, convents, etc.)
  Ideologically based political organizations and parties
  Hospitals
  Colleges and universities
  Social unions
  Voluntary associations and mutual benefit associations.
  Professional associations

Mixed structures
  Normative-coercive: combat units
  Utilitarian-coercive: some early industries, some farms, company
  towns, ships

---

and his group. Man is inherently lazy and must be controlled.
He is incapable of self-discipline and self-control. He is generally
untrustworthy, money-motivated and crafty. There are a few
exceptions to these assumptions—men who are trustworthy and
broadly motivated, and they must organize and manage the
masses.

This particular philosophy is well portrayed by Hampton
(1968). Hampton's examples of organizational behavior are

clearly based on assumptions of rational-economic man. He points out that organizations that view man in this way have almost absolute power over their personnel, made possible through incentives given to them. He argues that material incentives easily buy people in organizations and just as easily manipulate their behavior. Organizational power is virtually unchecked. Individuals in the organization are kept loyal through the use of bonuses and other "sweets," while the threat of their deprivation produces rigid conformity and obedience.

Social-man offers a view of man different from that of the rational-economic man. In this context man is basically motivated by social needs and seeks identity and meaning in social relationships. Hence, man is sensitive to his peers and their needs and is highly concerned with being liked and accepted by them. This makes man more in tune and responsive to social forces than to material incentives. A sense of belonging to the group is paramount in this philosophy of the nature of man.

Self-actualizing man as a model draws from the works of Maslow (1955, 1964), Goble (1970), Rogers (1961), McGregor (1960), Likert (1967), Argyris (1964), and others. The assumptions underlying self-actualizing man are that man's makeup falls into a hierarchy of needs, from the most basic needs concerned with physical survival of the organism to needs of the maximum use of his potential and resources, labeled self-actualization. In order of their strength and importance, the five needs of man are listed below. See Table III. As the lower order needs are satisfied, the higher order needs, in orderly succession, emerge and press for expression and gratification. When the physical, safety, and affiliative needs are met, even the most uneducated human being seeks satisfaction of the higher order needs.

Self-actualizing man is seen as self-motivated and self-controlled. He is capable of self-direction and craves autonomy and independence. He wants to be mature; he has an innate desire to improve. He resists efforts to externally control him and reduce his nature to a less independent state. Such external forces twist his essentially weak, but good nature. Fundamental to this philosophy of the nature of man is the belief that man is born good. Negative experiences in society are what twist and mangle man's

TABLE III

The Five Needs of Man

Higher Order Needs (5, 4)	5. Self-Actualization needs--the desire to utilize one's resources fully
	4. Esteem needs--needs for praise, rewards, importance, autonomy
Lower Order Needs (3, 2, 1)	3. Affiliative needs--needs for belonging and being accepted
	2. Safety and Security needs--essentially psychologically in nature; the need to feel safe, protected
	1. Physical needs--sustenance of life and survival of the organism

inherent goodness. This goodness never disappears, however. It is always there, ever ready to emerge under the right conditions.

Complex-man as a philosophy was developed because the other models of man were insufficient. Man is viewed as more complex than depicted in the other models. Complex-man is highly variable. In this view man is seen as having a hierarchy of needs and motives but these needs and motives undergo change from time to time and situation to situation. Complex-man can learn new motives and new needs as he interacts with his organization. Man's needs and motives can change from one part of an organization to another; from one organization to another. Man is too complex to fit any one model. He has all the models within him at all times. The model he utilizes depends upon the situation and needs and motives at the time he is behaving.

It is apparent that a philosophy of the nature of man is essential in determining the treatment man receives as a member of an organization. When observing the activity of many organizations often it is evident what a particular organization's philosophy of man is. Assumptions about the nature of man determine whether an organization treats its employees as trustworthy or untrustworthy, capable or incapable of self-direction, or respectfully. A philosophy of man predisposes organizational behavior to rather specific governing patterns. Unless the philosophy changes, the behavior within the organization is unlikely to change.

Higher Education and a Philosophy of Man

Higher Education is essentially concerned with the liberal education of men, and the organization of higher education has as its foremost purpose the accomplishment of this objective (Doenges, 1962). A long time observer of the scene of higher education has stated that the goals of higher education have but one aim, man; humanity itself (Gibson, 1964; Gibson, 1972).

Since man is the underlying purpose of higher education, it follows that a philosophy of the nature of man is essential to higher education. If man is seen as unable to control his feelings, untrustworthy, lazy, etc., then we can expect organizations of higher education to be quite authoritarian in their treatment of both students and faculty. If man is seen as capable of growth and self-direction and self-regulation, then we can expect to see higher education providing opportunities for students, faculty, and administrators to determine much of their own behavior. Much autonomy will be provided. There will be evidence of considerable trust.

Based on assumptions derived from a philosophy of the nature of man in institutions of higher education, students and faculty alike will either be restricted, constricted, constrained, little respected, distrusted, little utilized, and rigorously dominated; or autonomous, respected, trusted, sought after, rewarded and appreciated. An appropriate, healthy, positive philosophy concerning the nature of man must be selected.

Leaders in higher education and other organizations will do well to study the four models of man and select the one that appears to offer man the greatest opportunity to grow and develop and contribute his talents for the benefit of both the organization and society. Understanding these four models of man can give a manager the opportunity of deciding the model or models inappropriate for his organization. Without a philosophy of man, there is invitation for repression or chaos and confusion. With a philosophical base from which to draw, an organization will have a solid anchor from which it will be capable of measuring its behavior. Indeed, it will have a frame of reference with which to judge itself.

REFERENCES

ARGYRIS, C. *Integrating the Individual and the Organization.* New York: Wiley, 1964.

DOENGES, BYRON F. *A Theory of College Administration.* Bloomington, Indiana: Unpublished doctoral dissertation, 1962.

ETZIONI, A. *A Comparative Analysis of Complex Organizations.* Glencoe, Illinois: Free Press, 1961.

GIBSON, RAYMOND. *The Challenge of Leadership in Higher Education.* Dubuque, Iowa: Wm. C. Brown Company, 1964.

GIBSON, RAYMOND. *Block Grants for Higher Education.* Dubuque, Iowa: Wm. C. Brown Company, 1972.

GOBLE, FRANK. *The Third Force.* New York: Grossman Publishers, 1970.

HAMPTON, DAVID, et al. *Organizational Behavior and the Practice of Management.* Glenview, Illinois: Scott, Foresman, 1968.

LIKERT, RENSIS. *The Human Organization.* New York: McGraw-Hill, 1967.

McGREGOR, DOUGLAS. *The Human Side of Enterprise.* New York: McGraw-Hill, 1960.

MASLOW, ABRAHAM. *Motivation and Personality.* New York: Harper and Row, 1964.

MASLOW, ABRAHAM. *Eupsychian Management.* Homewood, Illinois: The Dorsey Press, 1965.

ROGERS, CARL. *On Becoming a Person.* Boston, Massachusetts: Houghton Mifflin, 1961.

SCHEIN, EDGAR. *Organizational Psychology.* Englewood Cliffs, New Jersey: Prentice Hall, 1970.

Some Differences Between Pro-Union and Pro-Company Employees

JOSEPH P. CANGEMI, M. EUGENE HARRYMAN
and LYNN FRED CLARK

The Edwards test was given to a group of essentially anti-company employees; subsequently, a group of pro-company employees was given the same test. A comparison of differing needs of both groups was undertaken. The results of this comparison of the two groups is presented herein with recommendations for implementing a program of activities, rewarding to each.

Several months ago, a large, Southern, rubber-based manufacturing organization provided a special course in human relations for its clock-card-type personnel. The course was offered by a professor from a well-known university. During the period of time that the professor was engaged in the course with these employees, he met with a group of them who voiced considerable contempt and disrespect for policies and procedures of the company. Utilizing as much tact and resourcefulness as possible, the professor asked if the employees would object to taking the Edwards Personal Preference Schedule, a personality test, so that he might better understand their needs. The professor remarked to the employees that he was very interested in understanding their needs and behavior in order that he might be in a better position to reflect them to the company. The employees agreed and subsequently the Edwards test was administered.

The Edwards Personal Preference Schedule is a psychological measurement instrument that has wide use in education, government, business and industry. The Edwards, as it is popularly called, is utilized in assessing 15 different personality needs of essentially normal individuals. These needs are *achievement*, the need for accomplishment and to do one's best; *deference*, the need to follow and conform; *order*, the need for organization; *exhibition*, the need for attention; *autonomy*, the need for independence; *affiliation*, the need for friendship and loyalty; *intraception*, the need to analyze the motives of oneself and others; *succorance*, the need for support and sympathy from others; *dominance*, the need to supervise, direct and lead others; *abasement*, the need to feel guilty and inferior; *nurturance*, the need to help others; *change*, the need for new and varied experiences; *endurance*, the need to persevere; *heterosexuality*, the need for experiences with the opposite sex; and *aggression*, the need to criticize, blame others and become angry.

The Edwards was administered to a group of 43 essentially hostile and negative employees who voiced strong dissent against the company. A group of 19 pro-company employees subsequently was selected by the organization and was administered the Edwards as well. A comparison of differing needs of both groups was undertaken. Various statistical procedures were utilized in the analysis of the data obtained. The results of the comparison of the needs of pro-union employees and the needs of pro-company employees follows.

When compared with pro-company employees, pro-union employees tended to be less motivated toward accomplishing objectives, toward doing their best and toward achieving things for the sake of doing them. They tended to complain more than pro-company personnel and seek more sympathy, emotional support, help and attention than the company-oriented group. When compared with company personnel, the anti-company group were more staunch, stubborn, somewhat hardheaded and found it more difficult than company personnel to give-in once they had made up their minds, regardless of ample evidence existing which could refute their point of view. When compared with pro-company people, pro-union personnel had a greater desire to be led. They also had a stronger need than did company personnel to be aggressive, to blame and criticize others, to be critical and to be vindictive. When compared with pro-company employees, pro-union personnel were more restless, more uncertain about what they wanted or wished to do and more often searched for new and different activities than did company-oriented employees because they could not seem to get interested long enough in what they were doing.

On the other hand, pro-company employees tended to be more interested in achievement and success, more interested in accomplishing things, more concerned with being recognized for their achievements and seemed to be more goal directed. They had a lower need to be critical, to blame others or to be vindictive than did union oriented personnel. They found it easier to compromise and behave conventionally than did union desirous employees. Pro-company people had a lesser need for sympathy, emotional support and attention than that required by pro-union laborers. Pro-company people were less restless, more content with what they were doing and were able to stick with their tasks until they were completed more than pro-union employees.

This, then, is a description of some of the essential differences in needs between pro-union and pro-company employees as seen by the employees themselves.

THE NEEDS ACCOUNTING FOR THE MAJOR DIFFERENCES

An additional statistical analysis was made to show which needs, of all the needs found to be important with regard to pro-union and pro-company employees, would be more discriminating than the others. This analysis determined that three needs tended to distinguish strongly between the pro-company/

pro-union groups. These three needs were achievement, endurance, and succorance. A more detailed explanation of these three needs is as follows (Edwards, 1953):

Achievement: To do one's best, to be successful, to accomplish tasks requiring skill and effort, to be a recognized authority, to accomplish something of great significance, to do a difficult job well, to solve difficult problems and puzzles, to be able to do things better than others, to write a great novel or play.

Succorance: To have others provide help when in trouble, to seek encouragement from others, to have others be kind, to have others be sympathetic and understanding about personal problems, to receive a great deal of affection from others, to have

---

PRO-COMPANY EMPLOYEES USUALLY POSSESS
THOSE PERSONALITY TRAITS ENDORSED
AND REWARDED BY MANAGEMENT

---

others do favors cheerfully, to be helped by others when depressed, to have others feel sorry when one is sick, to have a fuss made-over one when hurt.

Endurance: To keep at a job until it is finished, to complete any job undertaken, to work hard at a task, to keep at a puzzle or problem until it is solved, to work at a single job before taking on others, to stay up late working in order to get a job done, to put in long hours of work without distraction, to stick at a problem even though it may seem as if no progress is being made, to avoid being interrupted while at work.

Interpretation of the Findings

As indicated above, differences in needs existed between the pro-union and pro-company employees. These differences were utilized as the basis for developing a rationale concerning the reaction of employees toward unionization.

Pro-company employees, on the average, had a greater need to do their best and be successful (achievement). In addition, they had a greater need to work hard and complete their tasks (endurance). Both of these characteristics are the type endorsed and rewarded by management and organizations. It is likely, then, that these types of individuals will feel that the company supports them and they in return will be favorable toward the company. Also, these individuals may feel that unions are anti-company and therefore have unfavorable attitudes toward them.

Generally, pro-union employees had a significantly greater need for personal attention and sympathy (succorance). This is not a characteristic that is generally nurtured and rewarded in organizations. Quite the contrary, this characteristic is frequently an annoyance in a production oriented system. Therefore, when an employee makes an overt attempt to satisfy this need while in the job, instead of being rewarded by having the need attended to (being given attention in some way), the employee is likely to feel rebuffed or ignored and consequently the employee will likely feel that he/she has been punished. This would lead the employee to dislike and distrust the offending agent (the company). The action the employee takes to rectify the situation is likely to be an endorsement of the union. In this, the employee not only sees the possibility of having his/her succorance need met but, just as important, feels that he/she is able to strike back at the agent (the company/management). The union can capitalize on the situation and attract such employees by: (1) portraying the company as a heartless organization interested only in using human beings to make a profit for the company and insensitive to personal needs, (2) portraying the union as an organization that sympathizes with the employees and one that is sensitive

EMPLOYEES WITH HIGHER ACHIEVEMENT
NEEDS ARE MORE LIKELY TO FAVOR
COMPANY PROGRAMS

to their problems and (3) promising the employees a means whereby they can confront the company over grievances. Oftentimes a company promotes programs intended to increase employees' morale by rewarding employees that work hard and complete their production tasks. Employees with high achievement needs and endurance needs are likely to approve of such programs whereas employees with higher succorance needs might interpret the program as another means to "use" employees and reward "the favored few."

Company programs and actions are likely to be favored by employees with higher achievement needs and endurance needs. These employees tend to be pro-company. However, employees with higher succorance needs are likely to view company activities as abusive, threatening and unfair. These employees are likely to be anti-company. As a result of these anti-company sentiments, these employees are open to consider committing themselves to the organization that offers some strength and leadership with which to combat the organization they feel has treated them unjustly.

Turning Either Toward the Company or the Union

It is the impression of the researchers that, when compared with pro-company-type personnel, employees who have lower needs for achievement, lower needs for endurance and higher needs for succorance can turn either way regarding union membership. They can be persuaded either to side with the company or to side with that group which takes the strongest initiative to understand them, console them, counsel them, support them (emotionally), and accept them. Once it is determined who the individuals are that are demonstrating these needs, it is up to the

---

IT IS POSSIBLE THAT THE PRO-UNION EMPLOYEE COULD REGARD THE COMPANY AS THE IDENTIFYING ORGANIZATION

---

immediate supervisor to take the initiative to work with them in a positive manner because the imperative here is strong: either the organization finds a way to satisfy these employees and their particular needs or the organization that comes along (the union) and says that it will satisfy these needs, in all probability, will win the trust, support and approval of this group.

In the case of the pro-union employees in the particular company in which this study was conducted, the union came along, was not perturbed by the employees' poor work habits, made them feel more wanted, liked, accepted, confident, trusted, understood, cared for, etc., than they perceived the company did and, as a result, they committed themselves to an anti-company posture. If pro-company employees and supervisors would react favorably with anti-company personnel, then it is entirely possible that many pro-union type personnel could very well regard the company as the organization with which to identify rather than the union. Possibly, the organization that expends the most energy, the most consistent, year-long efforts at winning the confidence and trust of this group, is probably the one that will win their support.

Recommendations

Strong consideration should be given to the following examples of activities that employees, especially pro-union type employees, should find rewarding. Other activities could certainly be added to this list.

1. Front line supervision should spend more time listening to whatever it is that employees wish to talk about. Supervision must genuinely appear to be concerned; it cannot be just an act.

2. Supervision above the front line level should make every effort to pay some personal attention to employees, especially those with a high need for succorance, particularly when such personnel are working on the back shifts.

3. An employee oriented publication should be distributed with many newsworthy items concerning employees contained within it, preferably one with pictures of employees in it. No strong controversial messages from management should be contained in this periodical, as they would be perceived as threatening by pro-union type personnel.

4. More company sponsored athletic-recreational programs should be supported.

64

5. There should be consistent, periodic meetings with employees and management. Much praise and information should be incorporated into these meetings. Threats should be eliminated. Discipline should be handled privately and on an individual basis.

6. The company should support more outings on the part of employees and their families with supervisors mingling freely among them during such events.

7. More attention should be encouraged from pro-company employees toward seemingly pro-union employees. They should be friendly and accepting toward them. "We/they" attitudes should be avoided.

8. More frequent contact, especially visitations, by corporate management should be considered. Mingling with blue collar employees during visitations and imparting information and praise is highly recommended.

9. More communication from management concerning as many things as possible about the matter of work, progress, competition, the goals and values of the company, etc., is recommended.

10. An acceptable suggestions system should be designed, preferably with the help of the employees themselves.

11. There should be some designated individuals within the organization to whom personnel can go for help. The individuals could render direct assistance or might refer the employee to an appropriate professional person or community helping agency. The helping individuals should be made known to blue collar personnel, together with their area of interest and concern. They should have above average inter-personal skills and should be able to relate easily with all types of employees.

12. Disturbed personnel should be recommended to appropriate community agencies for help.

13. Blue collar personnel should be able to ask questions of anyone in the entire plant, without fear of punishment; they should be encouraged, however, to utilize the chain of command. They should also be permitted to ask whatever questions are on their minds.

14. Management should ask non-exempt personnel for input

(as much as possible) concerning decisions that have to be made that will effect them.

15. Those with the longest service and who have shown themselves to be loyal, dedicated employees should be rewarded whenever possible. This especially concerns visible rewards, such as promotions and job changes.

16. Front line supervisory positions should be filled with only the very best personnel available, especially those with good inter-personal skills. These are the most crucial and critical management positions in the company. Cold, arrogant, insensitive, mean, and unconcerned personnel should not be hired for such positions. They should be avoided.

REFERENCE

Edwards, Allen I. *Edwards Personal Preference Schedule.* New York: Psychological Corporation, 1953.

A Brief Psychology of Healthy and Unhealthy Organizations

Joseph P. Cangemi *and* DeWayne Mitchell

Working together accomplishes the major goals of organizations. Working apart usually impedes these goals. Individuals within organizations need to work in harmony. Organizations that do not achieve their goals and purposes generally are exhibiting some rather unwholesome symptoms.

CHARACTERISTICS OF UNHEALTHY ORGANIZATIONS

Many behavioral cues can be found within organizations that are having serious difficulties. Among them are much friction; much internal strife; much disagreement within on goals; lack of clear cut commitment on the part of both personnel and the organization; interpersonal rivalries; an apparent explosion brewing within; sagging initiative; a lack of healthy exchange of ideas; much fear in general; no faith in the leadership; fear of the future; no creativity; no trust in subordinates; subordinates do not feel free to discuss problems with their superiors; only occasional rewards are given; threats and much punishment; only top brass feel responsible; lower level personnel feel little responsibility for the organization and welcome opportunities to defeat it; information goes downward (rarely upward) and, when received, is received with much suspicion; little understanding or knowledge of the problems of subordinates; little interaction of staff, and always with fear and distrust; little teamwork; the bulk of decisions are made at the top of the organization—subordinates can say nothing; most things come as orders, never suggestions; organizational goals are overtly *accepted* but *covertly* are strongly resisted; control of the organization is concentrated strictly at the top (Bass, 1972; Deci, 1972; Feinberg, 1965).

Obviously, organizations with these kinds of problems will have little opportunity to meet their goals. They will be quite busy keeping their houses in order. They cannot worry about their ends; they have enough difficulties with their means. As a result, employees, managers, associates and organization image, etc., suffer considerably.

Jealousy is often a very strong motive that leads to organizational dysfunction. It is probably the greatest professional malice there is. Jealousy may have some positive benefits, but the harm it does more than offsets them.

POSITIVE PSYCHOLOGICAL DEVELOPMENT

Organizations must build and maintain a sense of positive personal worth and importance for the people who work within them. The most important principle here is the relationships in the organization, particularly the relationships between superiors and subordinates. These relationships must be supportive and ego building. The more often the superior's behavior is *ego building* rather than *ego deflating*, the better will be *his* effect on *organizational performance*. The following are questions which, when pondered, will strongly suggest an organization's orientation (Likert, 1967).

1. How much confidence and trust does the organization have in its personnel? How much confidence does its personnel have in it?
2. To what extent does the organization convey to its

personnel a feeling of confidence that they can do their jobs successfully? Does the organization expect the "impossible" and fully believe its personnel can and will do it?

3. To what extent is the organization interested in helping its personnel achieve and maintain a good income?
4. To what extent does the organization try to understand the problems of its personnel and do something about them?
5. How much is the organization really interested in helping its personnel with their personal and family problems?
6. How much help do personnel get from the organization in doing their work?

    a. How much is the organization interested in training its personnel and helping them learn better ways of doing their work?
    b. How much does it help them solve their problems constructively—not tell them the answer but help them think through their problems?
    c. To what extent is the organization interested in helping personnel get the equipment, etc., they need to do their job well?

7. To what extent is the organization interested in helping personnel get the training which will assist them in being promoted?
8. To what extent does the organization try to keep personnel informed about matters related to their jobs?
9. How fully does the organization share information with personnel about itself, such as its financial condition, earnings, etc., or does it keep such information top secret?
10. Does the organization ask for opinions of its personnel when a problem comes up which involves their work? Does the organization value the ideas of its personnel? Does it seek them and endeavor to use them?
11. Is the organization a friendly place in which to work? Are key people approachable?
12. Is the organization generous in the credit and recognition given to others for their accomplishments and contributions?

Obviously, too many negative responses will suggest serious organizational difficulties are taking place.

69

Before an organization can be developed to a point where it can assist its members to develop their talents as fully as possible, it must make some basic assumptions about people in general. In particular, it must make some assumptions about the people it influences and governs.

According to Maslow (1965), an organization should assume the following about its personnel:

1. People are to be trusted;
2. People are to be informed as completely as possible of as many facts and truths as possible;
3. In all people, there is the impulse to achieve;
4. Everyone will have the same ultimate managerial objectives and will identify with them no matter where they are in the organization or in the hierarchy;
5. There is good will among all the members of the organization rather than rivalry or jealousy;
6. Individuals employed are healthy enough; they are not psychopaths, schizophrenics, paranoids, brain injured, feeble-minded, perverts, addicts, and so on;
7. People have the ability to be objective and detached when required;
8. People employed are not fixated at the safety-need level (fear oriented);
9. Everyone has an active trend to self-actualization—freedom to effect one's own ideas, to grow, to try things out, to experiment and to make mistakes;
10. People can enjoy good teamwork, friendship, good group spirit, good group harmony, belongingness, and group love;
11. People can take it, they are tough, stronger than most people give them credit for;
12. People are improvable, but not necessarily perfectable; they can become better at what they do;
13. People prefer to feel important, needed, useful, successful, proud, and respected, rather than unimportant, interchangeable, anonymous, wasted, unused, expendable, and disrespected;
14. People prefer or perhaps even need to love their superior (rather than hate him); people prefer to respect their superior (rather than disrespect him);
15. People dislike fearing anyone;
16. People prefer to be prime movers rather than passive helpers;

17. People have a tendency to improve things, to straighten the crooked picture on the wall, to clean up a dirty mess, to put things right, to make things better, to do things better;
18. Growth occurs through delight and not through boredom;
19. People have a preference for being a whole person and not a part-person, not a thing or an implement, nor a tool or a "hand";
20. Human beings prefer meaningful work to meaningless work;
21. People prefer to be working rather than to be idle;
22. There is a preference for personhood, uniqueness as a person, identity in contrast to being anonymous;
23. People are courageous;
24. People have a conscience, they can feel shame, embarrassment, sadness, etc.;
25. People have the wisdom and the efficacy of self-choice;
26. Everyone likes to be justly and fairly appreciated, preferably in public;
27. Everyone, especially the more developed persons, prefers responsibility to dependency and passivity most of the time;
28. People get more pleasure out of loving than they get out of hating;
29. Fairly well-developed people would rather create than destroy;
30. Fairly well-developed people would rather be interested than be bored;
31. In fairly well-developed people there is a preference or a tendency to identify with more and more of the world.

SELF-ACTUALIZATION IN ORGANIZATIONS

An organization should help its people attain self-fulfillment or self-actualizing behavior; that is, growth in accordance with each person's capabilities.

Some characteristics that are observable of people within such an organization are as follows. A person in such an organization is more objective; sees things as they are; has accurate perception; judges people correctly; is more decisive; has a clearer notion of right and wrong; is more accurate in predictions; sees "through" things; has humility; listens to others; learns from others; is creative; is flexible; is spontaneous; has a willingness to make mistakes—desires to think; has openness; is willing to admit error and ignorance; can forget about himself and concentrate on others/on the job to be done; is self-confident; has self-respect; works hard; has a low degree of internal self-conflict; is well integrated; doesn't need to be protecting his ego continually; is well integrated, especially when facing challenges or when security is threatened; feels in *control* of himself and his destiny; has a good sense of humor; and lacks arrogance (Gibson, 1964; Goble, 1970; Cangemi, 1974).

ORGANIZATIONAL LEADERSHIP

Successful organizations require healthy leadership. Healthy leaders create a variety of positive conditions for their members. Among them are a mutual determination of goals; a chance to learn new things, to discover unusual talent; a chance to benefit society; an opportunity for advancement for all concerned; greater prestige and social status for both the organization and personnel, assuring more funds and making recruitment easy; a chance for *many* people to contribute, not just a few; increased autonomy; variety in work assignments; a chance to engage in more meaningful, enriching activities; more friendly, congenial associates; team effort; stability insured and sensed; a relationship of trust; a chance to influence products; increased opportunity for rewards; a growing rather than a decaying organization; and an integration of individual needs and organizational goals.

It is obvious that there can be many impediments to organizational goals. Once these impediments are removed and growth oriented attitudes and activities are assumed, it is entirely possible that movement in the direction of self-actualizing behavior may result on the part of many personnel. The environment will be healthier, and such an environment is required if human beings are to tap the tremendous potential for good they possess. Creating and maintaining this environment is the challenging task awaiting every organization, particularly those whose responsibility it is to serve the public and society.

72

REFERENCES

Bass, Bernard, et al. *Studies in Organizational Psychology*. Boston: Allyn and Bacon, 1972.

Cangemi, Joseph P. *Perceptions of Students, Faculty and Administrators Regarding Self-Actualization as the Purpose of Higher Education*. Unpublished Doctor's Thesis, School of Education, Indiana University, Bloomington, May, 1974, 106 pp. typed.

Deci, Edward, et al. *Readings in Industrial and Organizational Psychology*. New York: McGraw-Hill, 1972.

Feinberg, Mortimer. *Effective Psychology for Managers*. Englewood Cliffs, New Jersey: Prentice-Hall, 1965.

Gibson, Raymond C. *The Challenge of Leadership in Higher Education*. Dubuque, Iowa: Wm. C. Brown Company, 1964.

Goble, Frank. *The Third Force*. New York: Grossman Publishers, 1970.

Likert, Rensis. *The Human Organization*. New York: McGraw-Hill, 1967.

Maslow, Abraham, *Eupsychian Management*. Homewood, Illinois: The Dorsey Press, 1965.

Some Observations of American Management Personnel in Foreign Locations

JOSEPH P. CANGEMI

Each year thousands of Americans leave the continental United States to assume positions of one type or another in nations scattered throughout the world. Some secure employment as corporation presidents, while others obtain positions in lesser categories, such as repairmen, mechanics, welders, and plumbers, etc. Americans from all walks of life, and generally representing most of the trades and professions, embark annually on new careers, opportunities and adventures they are certain are awaiting them in their newly selected overseas homes.

But what about the conduct of these Americans serving overseas? What do North Americans sitting snugly in front of their fireplaces back in the United States, or glued to their television sets, know about the behavior of their representatives living overseas? The answer is undoubtedly very little, except perhaps for a few hazy concepts acquired from dashing through the pages of *The Ugly American*. Comments on the inappropriate conduct of the working North American citizen in cultures outside his own is the attempted topic of this paper.

UNHEALTHY MOTIVATIONS

The underlying motivations for wanting to leave the United States to work abroad on the part of those who do are not always psychologically healthy. We are well aware that, although motivations are not always easily diagnosed, they are always present. No one does anything without a reason. Sometimes the reason is unconscious and not readily known to the behaver, but nonetheless it is always there. Sometimes the motivation is simple; sometimes it is complex. The point is, although many North Americans are a credit to their country during their working tenure overseas, too many of them are a discredit to it because of their unwholesome deportment. These individuals are poor representatives of North American culture abroad and damage, sometimes quite seriously, its good reputation and status by their persistently unhealthy attitudes, conduct and social demeanor. Many of these unhealthy people were in need of professional psychological consultation before they left the United States. They merely transported their maladies with them. Foreigners often point to such characters as those who are opportunists, present day *dollar conquistadores,* ready and willing to grab and assume all they can acquire within the limits of the law. Respect and dignity for other persons while in the fulfillment of their acquisition needs is generally quite lacking. They are out for all they can get and they use all their faculties to this end. They are out to make their fortune, and it might prove quite unfortunate for anyone to attempt to point out their inappropriate, tactless, and distasteful practices. They usually hurt, and sometimes hurt badly (emotionally speaking), other human beings in the process, be they fellow North Americans or inhabitants of the host country itself. Such maladjusted personalities certainly can be found in the United States, but to find them abroad is disastrous, since their ego-centricity places their needs first and the needs of others second. Foreigners who encounter these types of North Americans are left with poor samples of typical Yankee behavior. One example of such behavior is the attitude on the part of many of these Americans that they are better than the people of the host country where they are living; that their culture is superior to those of other nations. Regardless of national origin or homeland, individuals who deliberately spout such ideas or demonstrate such attitudes to nationals of the nation in which they are residing are manifesting symptoms of poor mental hygiene.

FEELINGS OF INADEQUACY

Many Americans leave the United States for work abroad because they are plagued by feelings of inadequacy. They are afraid to compete with other Americans for better positions, better salaries, higher social status, and so on. They are convinced they can never satisfy the occupational-social goals they have set for themselves, which are oftentimes unrealistic. So, they head for developing countries where their technical skills and background make them "experts." Certainly there is no argument with individuals for seeking an opportunity in a foreign environment. Rather, the issue is with the resulting behavior of some of them, usually those of blue-collar status, after they reach the new environment. Once in the new country, and they observe cues of cultural differences and poverty, too many of them begin to assume an attitude of racial, national, and individual superiority to compensate for the strong feelings of inadequacy they possess. They often carry out these snobbish attitudes with educated nationals, even when these nationals are much better educated than they are. To add to the problem, many of these blue-collar workers, when they held jobs in the United States, held titles and positions of limited significance in the occupational prestige scale. For example, many of those working in industry were usually quite separated from engineers and others in the management-executive group, both occupationally and socially. However, with the great crying need that exists in many corners of the world today for skilled mechanics and other craftsmen, these heretofore lower occupational status employees are swept away by large American industries with equally large overseas holdings, transported bag, baggage and family to overseas operations sites, presented an expensive home, an impressive title with several men to command, and are given, by and large, a position in the occupational hierarchy of their foreign-located company they never before knew. This new feeling of greater self-esteem because of their worth to their company is unfortunately generalized to social situations *outside* their work hours and, in too many cases, leads to false attitudes of self-importance. For example, some mechanics who have the newly acquired title of General Manager of Automotive Maintenance, and an impressive salary to go along with it, have been observed to feel they are superior to the medical doctor, dentist, and engineer in social status, based principally on the fact that these people are non-American and their salary is lower than theirs. The more advanced, systematized knowledge, as Vance Packard calls it, of these professionals, means nothing to them. It is interesting to note that many of these same non-professional, magnificently titled American workers oftentimes snub North American professionals employed by their same company overseas, causing a good deal of friction—to say the least. The irony of this is that many of these native professionals have graduated from top universities in the states.

The following is another example of behavior worth recounting. An East Coast male, high school dropout, took a blue-collar job with a large American firm in a Spanish-speaking country. This individual worked approximately twelve years in this particular country, saved a large sum of money during the process and had luxuries and a standard of living unknown to a good portion of the American public. He was known to drink heavily and harbored strong feelings of inferiority. After more than a decade, this fellow still can't speak enough Spanish to communicate socially with nationals unable to speak English, and proudly voices his disposition on the matter by stating, "These people have to learn English if they want to talk to me." It isn't too hard to envisage the impression this gentleman has left on those who have had some contact with him.

Examples of inappropriate behavior of United States citizens who either are currently working overseas, have been there, or who are going there are countless. They are sad accounts of North American representation abroad. What these working Americans fail to understand is that they are as much ambassadors as are the regularly appointed Washington dignitaries serving overseas.

77

This author refers to these individuals as ambassadors because they should carry messages of good will and peace, if not through a foreign language then at least through their attitudes and deeds. Far greater impact do they have on world opinion than they realize, since the officially appointed government ministers rarely meet the public as they do.

THERE ARE A FEW

It is only fitting at this point that something be said on behalf of those healthier Americans who have worked overseas, or who are currently there, making an excellent contribution to intercultural acceptance and understanding. A profile of them might be something like the following. These individuals are quite flexible. They are highly optimistic. They attempt to learn the language of their new environment, no matter how poorly they end up speaking it. They continually try to improve it. They mix well with nationals and never look down upon them; they treat them as equals. They never get involved in political squabbles. Generally speaking, they carry themselves with an accurate and realistic sense of self-worth and dignity. Humility is something they seem to have in abundance. They are conscious of their social behavior and try to understand and enjoy the patterns and ways of the new culture in which they find themselves. They adjust to cultural conditions as they find them, rather than criticize them for not being more American-like. They never attempt to force American ideas. Instead, they demonstrate, when appropriate, American methods, tools, techniques, etc., without ever being offensive or distasteful. They even attempt to eat and enjoy native cooking. In short, these people attune themselves quite readily to their new environment. They do not expect nor want the environment to adapt itself to them. To say the least, these individuals are too few. Those few that do exist however, have a tremendous potential in their hands to build a solid, positive image of the United States abroad. The problem prevails in finding more of these types of mentally healthy, adaptable and flexible people to serve overseas.

PSYCHOLOGICALLY TESTING: THE SOLUTION?

The solution to solving the problem of whom to send overseas and whom not to send is, recognizably, not necessarily simple. But there is *something* that can be done. Psychological tests of personality and depth interviews might be given serious consideration for administration as an aid in selecting appropriate personnel before making decisions as to whom to send overseas. Consultant psychologists and psychiatrists might be contracted to do such testing and interviewing and then make appropriate recommendations. This is at least an effort that can be made to detect and shift elsewhere those applicants who show signs of emotional instability or, generally, a serious lack of mental health. Although such services might be considered costly, they are in reality trivial in comparison to the cost of transporting a man, his family, and his goods to an overseas assignment and then shipping them all back to the United States again because of emotional maladjustment or social unadaptability after only several weeks or months on the job. Although psychological testing cannot and should not be looked upon as the complete answer to the problem, it can offer tremendous assistance in the course of its remedy when handled by competent, well trained professionals.

Another approach to the problem is having a complete records and recommendations collection on file *before* making a decision or commitment to send an applicant to a foreign vacancy. Although this seems elementary, many firms and businesses, hard pressed to send needed personnel overseas, accept completely what solicitants say in their initial application for employment. Without receiving so much as one recommendation or verifying some of the data in their vitae, they hire these candidates and ship them to foreign locations at God-speed, sometimes only to regret the negotiation.

Last, a well planned, efficiently organized and sufficiently budgeted recruitment program is an essential requisite if success is to be obtained in securing the types of individuals who are good workers and at the same time satisfactory representatives of North American citizenry in transoceanic posts.

QUALIFIED PEOPLE EXIST

Highly skilled, technically qualified, well experienced, and mentally healthy individuals for overseas positions are available from the employment ranks of the United States. They do exist. Sending these types of individuals abroad will benefit greatly the image of the United States. Sending mentally unhealthy persons abroad can only damage it in the eyes of foreigners. Although many organizations do attempt to select not only qualified, but also psychologically healthy employees, too many concerns have not as yet arrived at such procedures. They continually *take chances* with their newly selected, foreign bound employees. Unless something is done to limit the number of psychologically unhealthy persons who leave the United States annually to work abroad, a hundred Santo Domingos will not be as damaging to our good name and reputation as will be the injury and impairment these individuals accrue each year as they continue to depart the country and, employment contracts in hand, take up years of residency abroad.

Peter's Principal Principle

JOSEPH P. CANGEMI *and*
KENNETH T. CANN

In dealing with human relations, we know that all individuals have specific assets and liabilities that generally determine the quality of job performance. Changed or increased responsibilities attached to promotions may, therefore, move an individual into a position in which he is forced to draw upon skills which are not among his assets.

An accountant, for example, may be promoted to an administrative position on the basis of past superior performance at handling numbers, balance sheets, and financial statements. The new position, however, may require him to utilize undeveloped skills related to meeting people, resolving human relations conflicts and participating in public relations activities. The former job was primarily related to numbers and things, whereas the new job is primarily people-oriented. If the man were more at ease with numbers than with people (this would not be surprising, as accounting, generally speaking, is a thing-oriented profession—Holland, 1966), then the new position would entail skill demands which are not consistent with thing-oriented abilities. If we accept Robin Marris' concept, as set forth in *The Theory of Managerial Capitalism,* that increasing responsibility

81

in hierarchical organizations means an increasing span of control over subordinates, we may conclude that promotion places greater demands upon human relations skills. Consequently, persons lacking those skills and talents may find themselves incompetent at higher level positions, even though performance was adequate at lower level positions. Competence at low level positions does not guarantee competence at high level positions. Figure 1 illustrates this point.

Moreover, it is not unrealistic to assume that individuals do not possess all of the skills and abilities necessary to perform all functions with equal efficiency. Because of differences in temperament, education, background and training, people tend to be proficient at a limited number of tasks. Given that natural division of labor, everyone is incompetent with respect to a wide range of possible tasks, and if given different assignments, will not be able to perform as skillfully as someone with specific training and experience in those areas.

A man may not be competent to handle a new job because he has not had the appropriate preparatory training. Industry obviously recognizes this and for that reason has established many and varied training programs, the main purpose of which is to

FIGURE 1

Skill Usage in Relation to Changed Position

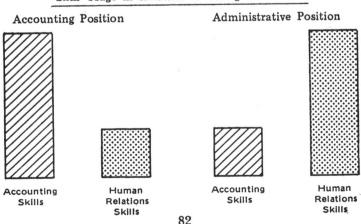

Accounting Position   Administrative Position

Accounting   Human   Accounting   Human
Skills   Relations   Skills   Relations
                    Skills   Skills

prepare people for the new or different responsibilities related to promotion. Individuals, therefore, may increase their assets and reduce liabilities with reference to specific positions through education and training. That does not necessarily mean, however, that everyone will display the same degree of on-the-job competence.

THE MODEL

Assume that the degree of competence required for each job position in a hierarchical organization can be determined, that there is a unique degree of competence associated with the duties and responsibilities of each individual position, and that competence position pairings are ranked in order on an ascending ordinal scale.

The model below is presented as a tool for interpreting the Peter Principle—the idea that it is inevitable for a man to reach a level of incompetence as he moves upward through a hierarchical organization. Figure 2 shows position ranks on the horizontal scale and corresponding competence ranks on the vertical scale. Position 1 requires competence of rank 1, position 2 requires competence of rank 2, and so on. The solid line OX connects all points at which competence rank equals position rank, other things being equal, and it may be called a required competence line.

Suppose a person enters a hierarchical organization at the lowest rank and gradually works up to higher and higher positions on the basis of seniority. If that person displays actual competence exactly equal to required competence for each position on the scale, he will move up through the hierarchy along line OX. He never displays incompetence or super-competence, but always functions at his competence plateau for each position.

A pattern such as that would not be inconsistent with Peter's thinking, but he would probably consider it to be rare. It presumes that the individual displaying such a pattern possesses the necessary inherent abilities, temperament, and background to function efficiently at successfully high positions involving different and perhaps more difficult skills and duties. It is possible that experience gained from on-the-job training might permit such a pattern to evolve. Peter claims, however, that every individual must eventually be promoted, unless he refuses, into a position at which he will become incompetent, i.e., he will not display the degree of competence required for the position. If such is the case, the individual's actual competence line will depart from line OX by branching off below it at some point in the hierarchy. Peter would probably say that people who remain on line OX have simply not yet been promoted to a high enough position to reveal their incompetence.

REACHING AN EQUILIBRIUM POINT

The more typical case may be represented by the dashed line CC, an individual's actual or displayed competence line. Given the stage of development of education in the United States, and the fact that most organizations require specific levels of minimum education as a prerequisite for employment, a newly hired

FIGURE 2

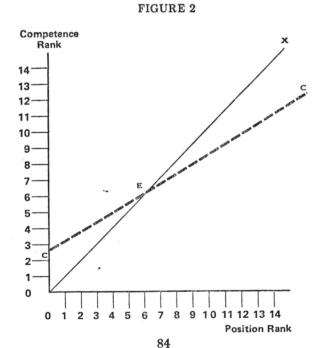

person taken into an organization at the lowest position may perform in a manner that is superior to required competence. That part of the dashed line to the left of E illustrates the case. It shows that the individual actually displays competence or rank 3 while working at position 1. As the person is promoted from position 1 up to position 6, his displayed competence increases by constant amounts, but not as rapidly as required competence. Since required competence rises at a faster rate than displayed competence, a position will eventually be reached at which both are equal as shown by point E.

Point E, then, is an equilibrium point showing a balance between position duties on the one hand and performance and efficiency on the other. The equilibrium point is equivalent to the person's competence plateau.

With promotions to positions higher than rank 6, the individual displays growing incompetence in relation to required competence for each successive position because marginal actual competence gains are still less than marginal required competence increases. To the right of point E the diagram shows an incompetence area formed by the open triangle XEC. The degree of incompetence for any position under the triangle may be measured by the vertical distance between actual competence line CC and required competence line OX. The individual is overemployed at any position of rank 7 or higher.

COMPETENCE PLATEAU IS THE EQUILIBRIUM POINT BALANCING POSITION DUTIES AND PERFORMANCE AND EFFICIENCY

To the left of point E an area of supercompetence is formed by the triangle OCE, and the degree of super-competence for any position under that triangle may be measured by the vertical distance between required competence line OX and displayed competence line CC. The individual is underemployed over that range of positions.

The position and slope of line CC are determined by the individual's prior preparation in terms of education, experience, personality, native abilities, background, and other factors, and none of these competence determining factors change as the individual moves along line CC and up the hierarchical ladder. As long as such factors are held constant, the individual must reach a competence plateau such as point E sooner or later. The model implies, however, that persons should be promoted as quickly as possible as long as displayed competence minus required competence is greater than zero. Otherwise, the organization will not maximize the competence returns for each individual.

An individual competence line such as CC reflects the behavior of one person, not groups of employees or other aggregations of people. Since individuals are not homogeneous with respect to the factors determining competence, it follows that there may be as many individual displayed competence lines as there are people. The origins and slopes of all possible CC lines will vary depending on differences in education, IQ, drive, temperament, ability, and attitude among individual persons, and the lines may be nonlinear as well as linear.

COMPETENCE PLATEAU MAY CHANGE

Although Peter does not stress the role of changing technology or of education and training in changing one's competence plateau, the model permits shifts to higher or lower levels of displayed competence in response to parameter changes. Suppose, as before, that an individual starts in the hierarchy at position 1 where he displays actual competence of rank 3. After successive promotions to higher positions, the person eventually reaches position 6 where displayed and required competence are equal. He has now reached his competence plateau. Further promotions will put him in a position where required competence exceeds actual competence.

Assume now that the individual perceives his limitations and decides to overcome them. Suppose he decides to improve his

---

INDIVIDUALS MAY INCREASE THEIR ASSETS AND
REDUCE LIABILITIES THROUGH EDUCATION
AND TRAINING

---

skills and abilities by means of additional education and preparation either through some kind of formal education or organization training program. If the person is intelligent and successful, the extra education and training will shift his displayed competence line to a higher level as shown by C'C' in Figure 3. With the person now functioning on a higher actual competence line, his competence plateau will also move upward to E' which corresponds to position 9. Some individuals may move to successively higher displayed competence lines, pushing their competence plateaus to higher and higher points along line OX, and never reach a level of incompetence. Others, however, may reach a competence plateau early in their careers, and never succeed in pushing it higher because of limiting factors such as inertia, satisfaction with present job, laziness, and lack of incentive and motivation.

Conversely, it is also possible that some persons may shift to

FIGURE 3

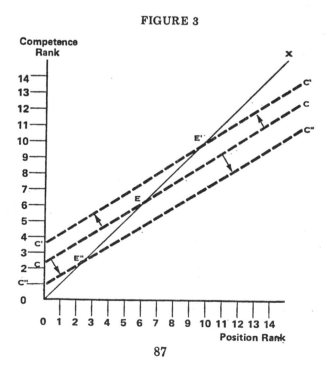

lower displayed competence lines, as illustrated by C"C". A downward shift may occur, for example, if the adoption of new technology requires different and possible superior skills and abilities from those currently required for specific positions and possessed by the incumbent. Suppose that position 6 is head of a bank bookkeeping department, and that the bank management decides to substitute computerized record keeping for hand bookkeeping. Although the ordinal scales do not change (competence rank 6 remains paired with position rank 6), the change to computerized bookkeeping raises the minimum skills and abilities required for position 6. The effect, therefore, is to make the department head incompetent at position 6 unless he quickly acquires knowledge of computer operations. The new technology pushes his actual competence line down to C"C", and lowers his competence plateau to E".

The model may be interpreted as showing that each person has a unique competence plateau in the short run. In order for each employee to make a maximum contribution to the organization he should, therefore, be placed at or promoted to a position consistent with his competence plateau, but no further.

Persons may, of course, be employed in positions less than the one consistent with the individual's competence plateau. In such a case, actual competence is greater than required competence, leaving a positive competence residual. Persons with positive competence residuals are not optimally employed. Others may be employed in positions beyond their competence plateau. Actual competence is now less than required competence, leaving a negative competence residual. These persons are also not optimally employed. Since at any given time some people may occupy positions above and others below their individual competence plateaus, the organization will not have an optimal, internal allocation of labor resources. In order for organizations to realize maximum returns from employed human resources, all personnel should be occupying positions at their competence plateaus.

CONCLUSION

This article was not designed to provide answers to the general question of why people are or become incompetent, nor has it attempted to supply reasons for human limitations or for the existence of ceilings on individual ability. Its only purpose is to provide a simple, general model to interpret Dr. Peter's hypothesis and thus stimulate further debate and testing of the Peter Principle.

REFERENCES

DARLEY, JOHN G. and HAGENAH, THEDA. *Vocational Interest Measurement.* Minneapolis: University of Minnesota Press, 1966.

DUBIN, ROBERT, HOMANS, GEORGE C., MANN, FLOYD C., and MILLER, DELBERT C. *Leadership and Productivity.* San Francisco: Chandler, 1965.

DUNNETTE, MARVIN D. and KIRCHNER, WAYNE K. *Psychology Applied to Industry.* New York: Appleton-Century-Crofts, 1965.

FLEISHMAN, EDWIN A. *Studies in Personnel and Industrial Psychology.* Homewood: Dorsey Press, 1961.

GILMER, VONHALLER. *Industrial Psychology.* New York: McGraw-Hill, 1966.

HAIRE, MASON. *Psychology in Management.* New York: McGraw-Hill, 1964.

HOLLAND, JOHN L. *The Psychology of Vocational Choice.* Waltham, Massachusetts: Blaisdell, 1966.

LITTERER, JOSEPH A. *Organizations: Structure and Behavior,* Volume I. New York: John Wiley and Sons, 1969.

MARRIS, ROBIN. *The Economic Theory of Managerial Capitalism.* Glencoe: Free Press, 1964.

PETER, LAURENCE J. and HULL, RAYMOND. *The Peter Principle.* New York: William Morrow and Company, Inc., 1969.

SUPER, DONALD E. *The Psychology of Careers.* New York: Harper and Brothers, 1957.

The Circle Concept of Leadership

GEORGE E. GUTTSCHALK

A great deal of personal conflict within an individual is attributed directly to the misunderstanding by that individual of his role in the organization as related to the authority, responsibility and control associated with his assigned position. This conflict results in unnecessary personal aggravation and contributes directly to inefficiencies, unnecessary costs and wasteful infighting. It is extremely detrimental to a manager of people.

If an attempt were made to define the designation of responsibility or appointment of authority in a typical organization, the time honored organizational chart usually emerges. A series of rectangles and connecting lines generally is visualized. See Figure 1-A. They descend from a solitary source, pyramiding down, multiplying by levels. Each level represents the considered height of responsibility. Each rectangle is an area of absolute authority. What many perceive is a theoretical blueprint which demonstrates the operational structure of an organization.

Unfortunately, the complexity of the organization and its competing activities does not allow it to function as it is so readily portrayed graphically. In reality, there is an overlap in the designation of authority and responsibility within a live organization which causes considerable frustration to those ranked

FIGURE 1-A

The conventional organization

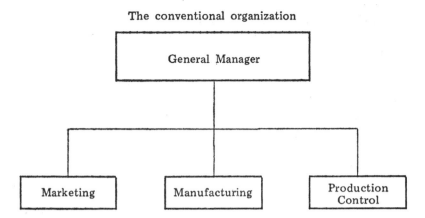

by the pyramid. Those who perceive the factors of authority and responsibility to be absolutely defined can suffer extreme frustration.

The *circle concept,* as a means of understanding the organization, portrays the organization as a series of overlapping spheres. Its design is two fold. First, it depicts mutual areas of control, and second, it relates to a General Manager's operating liberties. Each circle represents an area of activity and by nature of the overlap indicates the sharing of responsibility and authority. See Figure 1-B. Representative activities visualized are Production Control, Marketing and Manufacturing.

A simple physical example of an overlapping activity is the acceptance of a sales order by Marketing which is predicated on a determined delivery date. Here, in completing an accepted element of Marketing, Marketing exercises authority in two other activity areas. Marketing establishes both quantity and delivery date requirements in Production Control; Manufacturing commits its manpower and machining capabilities to this end. In either case, Marketing operates outside the scope of its recognized responsibility, yet in an operating organization, it is functioning in areas which it controls through overlap. See Figure 2. Conversely, if Production Control elects to postpone the delivery of

91

required material because of vendor scheduling advantages that re-establishes the delivery date, that is a development which originally was considered within the province of Marketing. Concurrently, Manufacturing may elect (for some legitimate reason) to revise its machining schedule to optimize the use of men and equipment. A third delivery date then would be established and in so doing overlap Marketing. Combination decisions can be made by any of the groups, affecting more than one other group.

In the example which was simplified for purposes of illustration, there are those who can, and will, unquestionably establish direct and positive responsibility and authority for these events. In doing so, they solidify their belief that each manager is the absolute governor of his "rectangle" within the pyramid. Any consideration of overlap is non-existent.

These areas of overlapping responsibility and authority within the complexity of a business organization penetrates each and every level within the organization. Understanding of this overlap by the individual manager allows him to function with great personal ease. Another key point in the recognition of this sharing of responsibility by various disciplines and their concomitant activity, as depicted by the overlapping circles, relates to the position of the controlling manager. Understanding the options

FIGURE 1-B

The Circle Concept

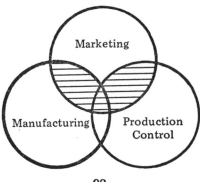

FIGURE 2

Manufacturing, Marketing and Production Control

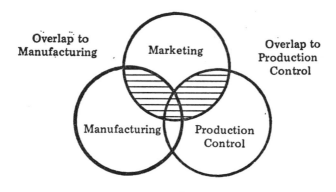

Overlap to
Manufacturing

Marketing

Overlap to
Production
Control

Manufacturing

Production
Control

Area of Combined
Decision Making

open to him in group management suggested by the circle concept of management allows him directly to dedicate a greater share of his available energy to achieving the defined objectives of the organization.

The striking advantages of the conventional organizational chart, as shown in Figure 1-A, is the definition of the General Manager's role. It appears as a straight line responsibility to defined functions. Unfortunately, it does not convey the activity of "molding" functional managers into a solidified operating unit; a group which, working intermingled as a team, will obtain maximum results.

In Figure 3, the dotted line represents the activity area of the General Manager. Drawing on his management expertise, he must determine the business maturity of his operating managers and their ability to group-interrelate. By management skill, he floats the circles, increasing or decreasing the overlap, to achieve maximum interplay based on the individual strengths or weaknesses of his managers. For him, the closer the circles the greater the overlap; the less "area of attention" requiring his concern. Reducing the "area of attention" permits him to focus sharply on

FIGURE 3

Activity Area of General Manager

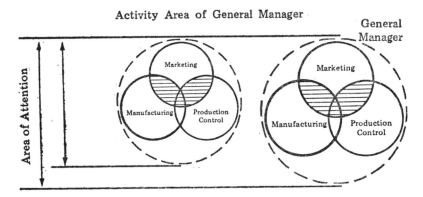

General Manager

selective problems. As the circles move apart, the greater the span of personal attention required on his part and the diluting of his efforts. The movement of circles can be carried to two extremes. If moved to a point of minimum overlap, because of personalities, a "zone of conflict" can be created. See Figure 4-A.

This inability of managers to function in a system of split responsibility can force the General Manager into a position of referee. The manager's greatest attention then will be directed to the areas of conflict between his managers which prevent him from adequately monitoring the total scope of both positions. Conversely, total overlap would be the total loss of discipline. See Figure 4-B.

FIGURE 4-A

Zone of Conflict

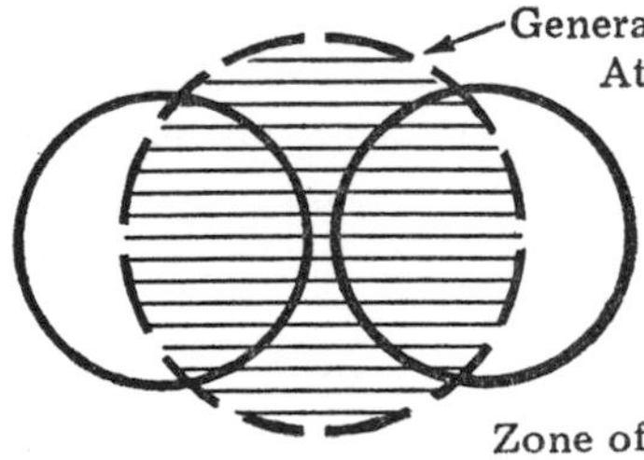

General Manager's Attention

Zone of Conflict

FIGURE 4-B

Total Overlap

The *Circle Concept of Management* relates to personal identity. Who we are, as related to the business organization and the participants within it, is critical to personal fulfillment. It offers a blueprint which, after understanding, can clarify the world of those working within the confines of the mythical pyramid.

Management Styles to Avoid

George E. Guttschalk *and* Joseph P. Cangemi

The authors have had substantial experience in the area of management, both as managers themselves and as consultants to hundreds of managers, spanning dozens of organizations: governmental, business, industrial, educational and military.

Based upon this experience, certain management styles have been observed which have led invariably to substantial problems and difficulties, both for managers themselves and for the organizations in which they were employed. Additional problems were created with considerable frequency by these management styles for subordinates whose role required responding to them.

One last observation: many managers whose administrative style essentially was composed of these behaviors in the long run were either demoted, frozen in their present position, shipped elsewhere, or simply were terminated.

MANAGEMENT STYLES NOT FREQUENTLY ASSOCIATED WITH SUCCESS IN DEALING WITH PEOPLE

The following management styles are those that should be avoided. They generally have not been observed to be associated with success.

The Dictator: He is *God;* he is always right. No other opinion counts other than his own. He manages by creating an atmosphere of fear. He is vengeful.

The Blocker: He blocks his employees from doing things that might get them noticed. He is afraid too much exposure of his subordinates might bring them opportunities that will lead to promotions, perhaps promotion over him.

The Withholder: He keeps information from employees; he doesn't want them too knowledgeable. He likes it that they have to depend on him for virtually all information. He enjoys and has a need to be the fountain of knowledge to his employees.

The Brownnoser: He got where he is by shining his superior's shoes and he knows it—and others know it. He looks for every opportunity possible to defer and accommodate to his superiors; to do extraordinary favors for them, sometimes to include spying on his peers.

The Butcher: His major objective seems to be to cut everyone up with his tongue. He never has nice things to say about anyone. Conversely, he enjoys pointing out the negative aspects of the behavior of others. He enjoys belittling, hurting, crushing other human beings.

The Non-Delegator: He has little faith in his subordinates. As a result, he does most everything himself. He has the unfortunate habit of assuming too much responsibility while his employees either crave for more responsibility or enjoy the inordinate amounts of free time caused by their superior's need to do everybody's work.

The Worrier: His major absorption is worrying about his subordinates, his superior, his company—most anything. He especially is plagued by the fear that he is going to be replaced. Sadly, if there is not much currently on hand to worry about he can be counted upon to search for something. He might even worry about someone else's problems.

The Troublemaker: He enjoys making people look bad. He especially enjoys finding others in the wrong, both subordinates and peers. Anything he can do to make the other fellow look bad, so that he can look well, is generally the aim of his conduct. He does others in so that, at their expense, he looks well.

The Malcontent: He appears not to have spent more than a precious few happy days with the organization since he joined it. He complains about everything. He sees only the negative aspect of things; he thrives on seeing what's wrong. He seems perpetually unhappy. Rarely will he quit, however.

The Weakling: His style is characterized generally by his inability to make a decision. He cannot, for the life of him, make decisions, especially difficult decisions. He would rather give in than make decisions that might cause him to be unpopular in the eyes of his subordinates. He does not seem to be able to muster up enough nerve to make the tough decisions all leaders are called upon to make from time to time.

The Jealous Executive: He appears jealous of others in every way. He is constantly over-observing what he has in comparison to other individuals. He finds it painful to see his peers, or even his subordinates and superiors, get more than what he has. From job title to desk size to office location, the jealous administrator usually is happy only knowing that others have less, much less, than himself. He dislikes seeing others move ahead.

The No Conscience Administrator: He is out for promotion, advancement, more money, etc., and he is not too concerned with how he gets them. If he has to step on people, lie, cheat, or even maybe steal to get ahead, then so be it. Getting ahead is the only thing that matters. How one gets ahead, and at whose expense, clearly is unimportant.

MANAGERS WITH UNCERTAINTY FEELINGS

Usually, managers and administrators who consistently exhibit these types of leadership styles are trying to cover up strong feelings of inferiority, inadequacy and uncertainty. They are too worried they will flop, that others will not respect them, that things will go wrong, that others will hurt them, or that they will look bad. They appear to concentrate and focus too much attention on what they do not do well, instead of concentrating on what they *can* do well and taking pride in it. They seem to have egos and accompanying feelings that bruise rather easily; criticism

98

of any type is out of the question. Because they do get hurt so easily, and because they are afraid of being either replaced, ridiculed or hurt in some way, they develop management styles which propel them to protect themselves. Hence, the styles mentioned in this paper.

This list was developed to assist managers in becoming more sensitive to their own management styles and the management styles of others.

Employee Theft and
Organizational Climate

WILLIAM L. TAYLOR *and*
JOSEPH P. CANGEMI

One of the most serious problems facing management concerns the reduction of internal theft. According to the Chamber of Commerce of the United States (CCUS) (1974), over 50% of those who work in plants and offices steal to some extent, with approximately 5% to 8% stealing in volume. In the same report, it was estimated that 60% to 75% of retail inventory shortages were attributable to employee theft. The yearly cost of employee pilferage has been reported to exceed by several million dollars the losses in the entire nation from burglary and robbery (Reckless, 1967). The cost of employee crime was summarized by the CCUS in its handbook on the subject.

> Internal dishonesty, in addition to the adverse effect on profits represented by the amount of pilferage or embezzlement, may result in costs associated with the loss of one or more trained employees; the training of replacements; higher insurance rates and/or deductibles; reconstruction of destroyed, stolen, or altered records; contamination of other employees who pick up where the apprehended thief left off; and lowered productivity when honest and valued employees feel they are under suspicion (p. 5).

Carl F. Frost (1974), an eminent organization consultant and proponent of the highly successful and innovative management technique, the Scanlon Plan, believes that employee behavior is a direct consequence of how he is treated; employees who are treated poorly will resort to aberrant behavior in order to gain attention, increase perception of self-worth, etc.

The purpose of this article is to examine internal pilferage and its relationship to organizational climate and the degree of employee alienation. It is the authors' contention that pilferage can be expected to increase as employees become alienated by cold, insensitive organizations and management styles, and that problem amelioration is only possible by eliminating the causes of worker discontent and maladjustment.

THE EMPLOYEE WHO STEALS

Since criminologist E. H. Sutherland (1940) began his study of white-collar crime, social scientists have attempted to determine the reasons why individuals engage in criminal behavior on-the-job (Clinard and Quinney, 1973). Unfortunately, there has not been a great deal of substantive work in this area. This can, in part, be traced to an absence of "conceptual clarity and consensus" regarding a definition of white-collar crime (Geis and Meier, 1977).

Much of the confusion can be traced to Sutherland's (1940) initial conceptualization of white-collar crime. He saw the phenomenon as being occupational crimes that were committed only by middle and upper class individuals. Quinney (1964) then proposed that the concept be expanded to include "all violations of criminal law that occur in the course of occupational activity." Subsequent research by Clinard and Quinney (1973) reflected that white-collar crime was in fact committed by all types of individuals regardless of their social class and that a distinction could be drawn between corporate and occupational crime. The former is criminal activity by corporate officials that is committed in the name of the corporation. On the other hand, occupational crimes are those that are committed by individuals for their own gain in the course of their occupation, with the employer as the victim.

101

Horning (1970) added the term "blue-collar" crime, which is criminal activity committed by nonsalaried employees against their employer. From Horning's perspective, white-collar crime includes both corporate crime and crimes by individual salaried employees who commit these acts against their employers. Horning's distinction between blue-collar and white-collar crime is important as it is the nonsalaried, wage earning employee that constitutes the larger portion of the work force and who, as a group, are more susceptible to pressures created by the work environment.

THE CAUSES OF STEALING—AN OVERVIEW

A number of studies have examined causation as related to individual weaknesses that predispose employees to be subjected to pressures that originate outside the organization. These include unusual family expenses, unsuccessful stock market speculation, and other forms of indebtedness. According to the CCUS report, however, this group of individuals is small when compared to the number of employees who steal while on the job because of various reasons *directly related to the work environment*. The CCUS document reflects that the larger group of employees steal because of on-the-job irritations, including:

> low and inadequate wage or salary, resentment against the company for alleged unfair or inconsistent policies, inordinately severe disciplinary actions, substandard working conditions, or a deep-seated feeling of not being appreciated by superiors (p. 55).

Preventive measures against those who steal because of some pressure from outside the organization consists essentially of routine security procedures that are applicable to any business, including inventory controls, employee pre-employment screening, access and egress control, etc. Preventive measures in the case of employees who are motivated to steal because of some problem internal to the work environment are much more complex. Not only must the individual be dealt with but, perhaps more importantly, the work environment and its relationship to the development of normative control measures must also be examined.

THE EFFECTS OF THE WORK GROUP

Clinnard and Quinney (1973) report that employees appear to accept or reject opportunities for occupational crime according to their orientation toward their roles and their social values. Horning (1970) conducted an extensive study of blue-collar crime in an electronics plant, the results of which revealed that each occupational setting contains its own set of norms concerning theft of company property. These norms were found to operate in the following manner:

> The work group subculture contains a set of norms which deal with pilfering in the plant. These norms, though necessarily vague, serve to provide the workers with a set of general guidelines relative to the acceptable modus operandi, the tolerable limits, the conditions of pilfering, etc.
>
> The pilferers of property are granted the protection of the work group only if they are pilfering within the tolerable limit. To exceed the limit is to risk losing the protection of the work group . . .
>
> The work group norms do not clearly delineate what constitutes a reasonable amount of pilfering (i.e., what constitutes a tolerable limit).
>
> There are, however, two broad guidelines: 1) what one needs for personal use and 2) that which will not jeopardize the system by focusing supervisory attention on the pilfering . . .
>
> In plants where pilfering does not assume the form of a protest, team pilfering is taboo because it violates the definitions of the tolerable limit . . .
>
> The work group norms of pilfering are assimilated through precept and work group folklore (pp. 63-64).

In all organizations workers tend to establish normative limits on the type and quantity of items that can be stolen. Even under the best conditions some pilfering can be expected, but in healthy

103

organizations with well adjusted employees, these losses can be expected to be minimal. In those organizations where the climate can be described as hostile and indifferent, employees have a low sense of job satisfaction and are, as a result, alienated (Saxberg and Sutermeister, 1976), which produces a situation that is not conducive to positive norm development and, therefore, higher rates of pilfering can be expected. In an organizational climate that fosters cohesiveness, group members will tend to adhere to norms that focus on facilitating the group's task performance activities rather than on maintaining interpersonal needs (Hackman, 1976).

ORGANIZATIONAL CLIMATE AND JOB SATISFACTION

The employee's attitude toward his job, including his perceived degree of job satisfaction, is directly related to the quality of climate within the organization. Davis (1977) states there is a high negative correlation between job satisfaction and other variables including employee turnover rates, absenteeism, waste, accident rates, etc. Locke (1976) reported from a somewhat different perspective that job dissatisfaction, alone or in combination with other factors, can have a variety of consequences on an individual's attitude and on-the-job behavior. These effects include the generalization of negative feelings toward others, poor emotional and physical health, excessive absences, and an increase in employee grievances. A worker's needs, goals and his state of job satisfaction influence his perception of the organizational climate; likewise, the organizational climate affects these same needs, goals and behavior (Payne and Pugh, 1976).

THE HEALTHY ORGANIZATION

In an organization that has a healthy work climate, employees have a high degree of job satisfaction and are motivated toward fulfillment of personal goals. Frost (1974) related that within a healthy organization employees "develop significant and interdependent relationships in promoting goals compatible with the organization's needs," and that employees become "innovative and responsible in achieving satisfactions consistent with the organization's requirements and achievements." As employees identify closely with the organization, employee behavior is functional in relation to the goals of the organization.

In organizations where the employee's and the organization's goals and objectives are congruent and mutually supporting, work group norms are clearly defined. In those instances, pilferage beyond the normative limits will be severely sanctioned by the work group, as stealing from the organization is seen the same as stealing property from a fellow worker, which is a taboo.

THE UNHEALTHY ORGANIZATION

In unhealthy organizations, individual needs and organizational goals are divergent, and are counterproductive to each other. This conflict disrupts group unity, diverts attention from collective goals, and leads to increased bitterness and alienation (Horton and Hunt, 1968). This type of alienation was forecasted by Karl Marx as a consequence of capitalism. Alienation is a process wherein individuals retreat from active involvement with others and tend to reject group norms (Reckless, 1967).

Seeman (1959) identified five aspects of alienation which can be used to explain employee behavior in unhealthy organizations. When employees are alienated, they develop feelings of isolation, powerlessness, meaninglessness, self-estrangement, and normlessness. Isolation can be seen in the employee's rejection of the organization's goals and objectives. To work toward the organization's objectives would require that the employee completely subvert his own needs and goals. To work toward his own goal fulfillment at the exclusion of those of the organization would be difficult, if not impossible, and would most likely result in the employee being dismissed. As either situation is unsatisfactory, isolation or retreat at least provides some relative sense of security and does not require a decision between two unacceptable alternatives.

When alienated, a feeling of powerlessness develops and employees do not see the relationship between their behavior and the success or failure of the organization. A general sense of

105

confusion and ambiguity tends to characterize organizations in which employees are highly alienated. Employees are not able to obtain a clear picture of where they are or where they or the organization are going. The work environment is so ambiguous that it becomes meaningless. As the realization of self-satisfaction and a sense of achievement is most difficult to obtain in an unhealthy organization, employees experience a great deal of self-estrangement and become antagonistic and cynical.

Alienation leads to a generalized condition of normlessness, where social control of behavior is ineffective and employees often feel it takes unapproved behavior to satisfy their needs and reach their goals. Indeed, a great deal of this behavior can be seen as a method of getting back at the organization and as a means of venting frustration and hostility.

CONCLUSION

Horning (1970) found clear evidence that workers' attitudes were a function of the perceived attitudinal milieu in the organization. If the organizational climate is seen as cold, withdrawn and impersonal, the workers will mirror that attitude. As one would expect, Nettler (1959) found that admitted criminal activity was positively correlated with the degree of individual alienation. *The evidence does seem to suggest that unhealthy organizations tend to alienate employees, which results in a reduced normative control of behavior and can lead to higher pilferage rates and other aberrant behavior, which is obviously very costly.*

REFERENCES

CHAMBER OF COMMERCE OF THE UNITED STATES. *A Handbook on White Collar Crime.* Washington: Chamber of Commerce, 1974.

CLINARD, M. B. and QUINNEY, R. *Criminal Behavior Systems,* 2nd ed. New York: Holt, Rinehart and Winston, 1973.

DAVIS, K. *Human Behavior at Work,* 5th ed. New York: McGraw-Hill, 1977.

FROST, C. F., WAKELEY, J. H. and RUH, R. A. *The Scanlon Plan for Organization Development: Identity, Participation and Equity.* Michigan State University Press, 1974.

GEIS, G. and MEIER, R. F., eds. *White Collar Crime,* revised ed. New York: The Free Press, 1977.

HACKMAN, J. R. Group Influences in Individuals. In M. D. Dunnette (Ed.), *Handbook of Industrial and Organizational Psychology*. Chicago: Rand McNally, 1976.

HORNING, D. N. M. Blue Collar Theft: Conceptions of Property, Attitudes Toward Pilfering, and Work Group Norms in a Modern Industrial Plant. In E. O. Smigel and H. L. Ross (Eds.), *Crimes Against Bureaucracy*. New York: Van Nostrand Reinhold, 1970.

HORTON, R. B. and HUNT, CHESTER L. *Sociology*, 2nd ed. New York: McGraw-Hill, 1968.

LAWLER, E. E. Critical Systems in Organizations. In M. D. Dunnette (Ed.), *Handbook of Industrial and Organizational Psychology*. Chicago: Rand McNally, 1976.

LOCKE, E. A. Nature and Causes of Job Satisfaction. In M. D. Dunnette (Ed.), *Handbook of Industrial and Organizational Psychology*. Chicago: Rand McNally, 1976.

MEIER, D. L. and BELL, W. Anomia and Differential Access to Achievement Goals. *American Sociological Review*, Vol. 24, No. 2 (1959) pp. 189-202.

NETTLER, G. Antisocial Sentiment and Criminality. *American Sociological Review*, Vol. 24, No. 2, (1959), p. 207.

PAYNE, R. and PUGH, D. S. Organizational Structure and Climate. In M. D. Dunnette (Ed.), *Handbook of Industrial and Organizational Psychology*. Chicago: Rand McNally, 1976.

QUINNEY, R. The Study of White Collar Crime: Toward a Reorientation in Theory and Research. *Journal of Criminal Law, Criminology and Police Science*, Vol. 55, (1964), pp. 208-214.

RECKLESS, W. C. *The Crime Problem*, 4th ed. New York: Appleton-Century Crofts, 1967.

SAXBERG, B. O. and SUTERMEISTER, R. A. Humanizing the Organization: Today's Imperative. In H. Meltzer and F. R. Wickert (Eds.), *Humanizing Organization Behavior*. Springfield, Illinois: Charles C Thomas, 1976.

SEEMAN, M. On Meaning of Alienation. *American Sociological Review*, Vol. 24, No. 6 (1959), pp. 785-790.

SUTHERLAND, EDWIN, H. White-Collar Criminality. *American Sociological Review*, Vol. 5, No. 1 (1940), pp. 1-12.

U.S. DEPARTMENT OF COMMERCE. *Crime in Service Industries*. Washington: Department of Commerce, 1977.

Awareness: A Psychological Requisite for the Well Developed Personality*

Joseph P. Cangemi *and*
Carl R. Martray

James Coleman (1964) has labeled the Twentieth Century the Age of Anxiety. Physical threats no longer plague man as they once did in the past. Instead, worries, doubts, conflicts, loneliness, disenchantment, disillusionment, etc., have arisen to take their place. In spite of the wealth of available literature and knowledge regarding mental illness, more than one half the hospital beds in the United States continue to be occupied by those who have serious emotional problems (Millon, 1970). Emotional problems continue to incapacitate more people annually than all other health problems combined. Due to the fast-paced, anxiety provoking existence of the Twentieth Century, problems of attaining and maintaining sound mental hygiene challenge everyone everyday.

---

* The editors have included this and the next article because of their emphasis on human growth and development and their implications regarding humanistic management in organizations.

108

AWARENESS: THE FOUNDATION OF
PSYCHOLOGICAL SURVIVAL

The key to psychological survival in this tension oriented age is awareness: awareness of self, awareness of others, and awareness of the world around us. Self-awareness appears to be the most important awareness the organism can attain. It is strongly related to positive mental well being, and positive mental well being is necessary in order to utilize one's capacities to the fullest (Maslow, 1964).

According to Barksdale (1972), self-awareness is not easy to attain. Few people are *really* aware of how they feel about themselves, and hence are relatively unaware regarding others and the environment. Barksdale attributes this to the natural desire to accept only positive characteristics about oneself while rejecting negative traits. Individuals who refuse to take rational, objective views of themselves generally have correspondingly low opinions of themselves. Because of this, inner peace becomes hard to attain. High self-regard results from accepting responsibility for one's behavior and then, because of this awareness, taking charge of one's life. Those with low self-awareness, who are not aware of and who do not understand their actions, needs, thoughts, and inner urges, are generally filled with a debilitating sense of inferiority, inadequacy and inner turmoil that prevents them from functioning in an effective manner (Barksdale, 1972).

THE VALUE OF SELF-AWARENESS

Self-awareness helps the individual to free his intelligence so that he can deal rationally, objectively, and effectively with himself and the environment. Self-awareness helps the individual to understand his own psychological needs and makeup and how to meet them, thereby making it possible for him to become more aware of the psychological needs and makeup of those around him. Self-awareness also acts in a preventative manner by helping the individual to meet successfully circumstances and situations in which his mental hygiene might be endangered. At the same time, this allows him to become aware of circumstances and situations which endanger the mental hygiene of others (Redl and Wattenberg, 1959).

People appear to show concern about their psychological well being. The more knowledge they have about themselves the better equipped they tend to be with regards to handling their own questions and concerns. The inability to deal rationally and intelligently with one's own questions and behavior predisposes him to be unable to react intelligently and rationally to the behavior of others. This state of affairs can lead to intense anxiety.

Self-awareness has the potential of making life better. It can help individuals be happier, more stable, and more confident. It is essential to the growth and development of the human organism. A review of the literature finds many individuals concerned with self-awareness. For example, Glasser (1969) has written that human beings have but one basic need, identity. There can be no identity without self-awareness. Without a strong sense of identity, being sensitive and aware of the identity of others becomes virtually an impossibility. Coppersmith (1967) wrote that self-awareness was imperative to good self-esteem. Without a strong foundation of self-awareness, developing a high degree of self-esteem would not be possible. The lack of high self-esteem for oneself negates the potential of developing a high degree of awareness and esteem for others. Coopersmith pointed out that without a high degree of self-awareness there could be no consistent expectation of one's own behavior. Without a high degree of self-awareness the individual generally lacks the appropriate trust and confidence he needs in himself and in his talents. This lack of self-awareness seems to inhibit the ability to consistently predict the very behavior one possesses. This, then, carries over and negates the opportunity to predict the behavior of others with consistency.

Self-awareness is highly related to a high degree of self-respect (Carroll, 1969). According to Carroll, a good sense of self-awareness generally develops into a high degree of self-regard, and high self-regard is essential for a positive state of mental hygiene. A person with a good sense of self-awareness generally has a positive view of himself, which permits him to have a positive view

110

of others, which then permits him to have an accurate awareness and perception of the environment around him. As a result of this positive self-view, the individual generally is free from threat to his perception of himself, resulting in low level anxiety. The need to develop elaborate psychological defenses against potential threats to one's self-esteem likewise becomes unnecessary. Because of the development of a high level of self-awareness and the resulting high level of awareness of others, the denial of the realities of life becomes unimportant. The organism seems able to cope with what is perceived. On the contrary, difficult circumstances are accepted and handled well and do not lead the individual to a state of serious depression. They do not bring the organism to a halt. There is no attempt to distort reality; it is perceived as it is, accepted and adjusted to without undue difficulty or strain.

SELF-ACCEPTANCE AND SELF-ACTUALIZING BEHAVIOR

According to Samler (1960), the mentally healthy individual accepts himself and likes himself. Liking oneself and accepting oneself frees the individual to accept others and live harmoniously with them. It also helps him to deal more effectively with the environment. Many behavioral scientists have agreed that self-awareness is a most important part of the healthy individual's pattern of growth and development (Maslow, 1954; Fromm, 1955, 1956; Reisman, 1955; Shaffer & Shoben, 1956; Shoben, 1957; Rogers, 1961). Essentially, these writers have stated that the healthy person is aware of himself, accepts himself, becomes aware of others, accepts others, lives harmoniously with the environment, and accepts responsibility for the consequences of his own choices and actions.

Self-acceptance affects the degree of self-insight an individual attains (Keezer, 1971). Individuals who have attained a good level of self-acceptance do not seem to be afraid to admit weaknesses and error, or incur the disapproval of others. Acceptance of oneself is important to daily productivity. Those who have accepted themselves do not waste energy protecting their egos

111

from others. Consequently, they have more energy and are more open to become creative and social (Goble, 1970).

Grebstein (1969) wrote that self-acceptance permits the individual to deal with the world around him objectively. Because of this acceptance of the world around him, the individual is now open to new experiences and does not develop unnecessary or unmanageable anxiety when faced with esteem threatening encounters. A poor sense of self-acceptance conditions the organism to self-protecting behavior. The need for self-protection restricts the individual from seeking new experiences which would have the potential of helping him develop many of his capacities to their fullest. New experiences are avoided because they represent too much threat. Behind this fear of new experiences generally can be found *a fear of failure*. Fear of failure generally inhibits the organism from interaction with others and the environment. A high level of self-awareness can help the individual accept failure without undue harm to self-esteem (Lindgren, 1969).

Self-awareness can be determined by observing the way an individual responds to others. Since self-awareness is related to self-acceptance, the individuals who hold themselves in high regard are other-directed. Other-directed individuals are more aware of the needs of others. Because of his self-knowledge, self-understanding, self-acceptance, and improved self-esteem, the individual can give of himself, put others at ease and, in general, contribute positively to interpersonal relationships and environmental harmony. Low self-regard directs behavior in a negative way. Individuals with low self-awareness have little to give of themselves, are selfish, egocentric, and are self-gratifying in their interpersonal conduct. They use people mainly to satisfy their own selfish needs and impulses. They are unable to tolerate circumstances and situations which do not bolster their own impoverished sense of self-worth.

Low level self-regard and low-level self-awareness are strongly related (Ringness, 1969; Keezer, 1971). There can be no mental hygiene without high regard for oneself; and without high regard for oneself there cannot be high regard for others. Without high regard for oneself and others, the environment becomes a source

112

FIGURE I

From Self-Awareness to Self-Actualizing Behavior: A Model

(The Process: Self-Awareness → Insight → Self-Understanding →
Self-Acceptance → Psychological Growth → Mental Health →
Self-Actualizing Behavior → Self-Awareness)

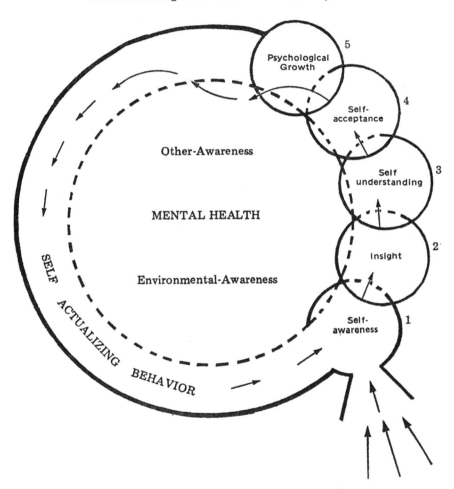

of consistent conflict. In summation, high self-esteem is dependent upon self-acceptance. Acceptance of oneself leads to acceptance of others. Acceptance of oneself and others nourishes a healthy adjustment to the environment. These behaviors are dependent fully on self-awareness.

FROM SELF-AWARENESS TO SELF-ACTUALIZING BEHAVIOR: A MODEL

According to this model (see Figure 1), self-actualizing behavior rests heavily upon self-awareness. Self-awareness leads the individual to substantial insight about his behavior, which leads him to understanding and accepting his own behavior, thereby moving him towards psychological growth. Psychological growth then leads the individual to a high degree of awareness of the behavior of others and the environment. Through these unfolding behaviors the individual develops mental hygiene. From this state of mental hygiene the individual unfolds further and self-actualizing behaviors start pressing upon him for expression. That there is a strong relationship between self-awareness and self-actualizing behavior seems more than reasonable.

In sum, the authors have sought to develop a model for viewing a process leading to self-actualizing behavior.*

REFERENCES

BARKSDALE, L. S. *Building Self-Esteem.* Los Angeles, California: The Barksdale Foundation for Furtherance of Human Understanding, 1972.
CANGEMI, J. and ENGLANDER, M. From self-awareness to self-actualization. *College Student Journal,* 1974, Vol. 8, No. 3, April-May 1974, pp. 88-92.
CARROLL, H. A. *Mental Hygiene.* Englewood Cliffs, New Jersey: Prentice-Hall, 1964.
COLEMAN, J. *Abnormal Psychology and Modern Life.* Glenview, Illinois: Scott Foresman, 1964.
COOPERSMITH, S. *Antecedents of Self-Esteem.* San Francisco, California: W. H. Freeman, 1967.
FROMM, F. *The Art of Loving.* New York: Harper & Row, 1956.
GLASSER, W. *Schools Without Failure.* New York: Harper & Row, 1969.
GOBLE, F. *The Third Force.* New York: Grossman Publishers, 1970.

---

* This model modified an earlier version of the process developed by Cangemi and Englander (1974).

114

GREBSTEIN, L. *Toward Self-Understanding.* Glenview, Illinois: Scott, Foresman and Company, 1969.

HOLLAND, J. *The Psychology of Vocational Choice.* Waltham, Massachusetts: Blaisdell Publishing Company, 1966.

KEEZER, W. S. *Mental Health and Human Behavior.* Dubuque, Iowa: Wm. C. Brown Company, 1971.

LINDGREN, H. C. *Readings in Personal Development.* New York: American Book Company, 1969.

MASLOW, A. *Motivation and Personality.* New York: Harper & Brothers, 1954.

MILLON, T. *Modern Psychopathology.* Philadelphia: W. B. Saunders Company, 1970.

REDL, F. and WATTENBERG, W. *Mental Hygiene in Teaching.* New York: Harcourt, Brace and World, 1959.

REISMAN, D. *The Lonely Crowd.* New York: Doubleday and Company, 1955.

RINGNESS, T. A. *Mental Health in the Schools.* New York: Random House, 1969.

ROGERS, C. R. *Client-Centered Therapy.* New York: Houghton Mifflin, 1961.

SAMLER, J. *Basic Approaches to Mental Health.* Washington, D. C.: American Personnel and Guidance Association, 1960.

SCHEIN, E. *Organizational Psychology.* Englewood Cliffs, New Jersey: Prentice-Hall, 1970.

SHAFFER, L. F. and SHOBEN, J. E. *The Psychology of Adjustment.* Boston: Houghton Mifflin Company, 1956.

SHOBEN, E. J. Toward a concept of the normal personality. *American Psychologist,* 1957, Vol. 12, No. 4, pp. 183-189.

Characteristics of Self-Actualizing Individuals

Joseph P. Cangemi

Individuals who are either moving toward self-actualization or who have achieved self-actualizing behavior have many positive characteristics. Among them are the following.

They have superior judgment and wisdom. They see through the superficial characteristics of people and see the genuine selves. They are able to share friendship with others, regardless of race, creed, color, and social standing. They tolerate the shortcomings of others. They see things freshly and without prejudgment. They have less confusion about what is right and wrong, good and bad. They see easily the good and evil in each situation. They have more accurate predictive abilities. They are problem centered and are concerned with ends, not means. They are less emotional. Their perception is superior. They prefer good values and develop them easily. They have an inner core of principles and character traits.

They are in control of their destiny and are sure of themselves. They feel strong, self-sufficient, confident and have a low degree of internal self-conflict; they have a high degree of self-respect. They have high respect for others. They have little fear of themselves or their desires. They have a good understanding of themselves and have a high degree of self-awareness. They have a good sense of humor. They are able to postpone pleasure for greater fulfillment. Their feelings of adequacy are based on their strengths and their accomplishments, in spite of their failures and weaknesses. They are courageous and willing to make mistakes. They have a great desire to help the human race and are able to further their own interests while at the same time furthering the interests of society. They have a healthy respect for themselves and are more open, flexible and humble. They are constructively critical.

They develop intimate relationships with others, unencumbered by expectations and obligations. They enjoy doing good for others and take pleasure in rewarding, praising, and recognizing the talents of others. They enjoy the good qualities of others and are able to accept their faults. They are other-directed and are concerned with the problems of others.

They have a more integrated and harmonious personality. They have their problems under control to the point they can work on the problems of the community and society. They do not expend all energies working out their own problems. They are able to concentrate well. They become highly integrated when facing a challenge. They have broadened interests and are highly creative. They are spontaneous, expressive, natural, free. They are more simple and get more out of life. They appreciate life more and live more fully in the here and now. They never tire of life and enjoy living. They are more aware of the environment and appreciate the beauty around them.

They are reliable, trustworthy and dependable. They are little threatened by the unexpected, and tend to be less inflexible and rigid in the face of uncertainty. They are not threatened by differences, especially differences in others. The mysterious, unknown, and the environment do not threaten them. They are not threatened by themselves. They have confidence they can handle whatever confronts them. They have a sense of trust, goodness, and beauty and have a sense of kinship with the whole human race.

They become committed to important jobs and tasks and do

117

them well. They enjoy responsibility and find it rewarding. They work hard. They enjoy work so much they tend to see it as play. They develop their vocational potential in accordance with their personality and needs. They view work as exciting and pleasant. They enjoy problem solving and find satisfaction in making order out of chaos.

They are highly independent. They are especially unconventional when their basic principles are endangered. They forego popularity and stand up for their beliefs. They have and need autonomy, are self-sufficient, are individualistic, and are inner directed. They are independent, yet can enjoy relationships with other people. They have a healthy desire and respect for people yet rely fully on themselves and their own capacities. They are governed by their own inner directions, their own nature and their own needs, rather than the dictates of society or the environment. They make their own decisions, even in the face of controversies and popular opinion. They maintain their own points of view and are not swayed easily. They have peak experiences often.

In short, they are fully human, fully functioning, and have developed their capacities to their fullest. They have uncovered and developed their uniqueness. They have become what they can become. They have evolved their latent or existing potential. They have learned what is and is not possible and have taken the appropriate steps to develop what is possible.

REFERENCES

ALLPORT, G. W. The Ego in Contemporary Psychology. *Psychological Review,* 1943, *50,* 451-478.

COOMBS, A. W. and SNYGG, D. *Individual Behavior.* New York: Harper Brothers, 1969.

GOBLE, F. *The Third Force.* New York: Grossman Publishers, 1970.

GOLDSTEIN, K. Health as Value. In Abraham H. Maslow (Ed.), *New Knowledge in Human Values.* Chicago: Henry Regnery Company, 1959.

KELLY, E. C. The Fully Functioning Self. In *Perceiving, Behaving, Becoming.* Yearbook of the Association for Supervision and Curriculum Development. Washington, D.C.: National Education Association, 1962.

MADDI, S. R. *Perspectives on Personality.* Boston: Little, Brown, and Company, 1971.

MASLOW, A. H. *Motivation and Personality.* New York: Harper Brothers, 1954.

Maslow, A. H. *The Farther Reaches of Human Nature.* New York: The Viking Press, 1971.

Rogers, C. R. *Counseling and Psychotherapy.* New York: Houghton Mifflin Company, 1942.

Rogers, C. R. A Theory of Therapy, Personality, and Interpersonal Relationships, as Developed in the Client-Centered Framework. In Sigmund Koch (Ed.), *Psychology: A Study of a Science,* Vol. 3. New York: McGraw-Hill Book Company, Inc., 1961.

Rogers, C. R. Toward a Science of the Person. *Journal of Humanistic Psychology,* 1963, *3*, 72-92.

Sutich, A. J. The Growth-Experience and the Growth-Centered Attitude. *Journal of Psychology,* 1949, *28*, 293-301.

Voeks, V. *On Becoming an Educated Person.* Philadelphia: W. B. Saunders Company, 1970.

Management's Challenge: A Changing Value System

RICHARD A. HEADLEY

In his book, *Psychological Man,* Dr. Harry Levinson contends that "as much as eighty percent of executive failure is due to the inability to lead, motivate and integrate *people* toward the achievement of common purpose." Without quibbling about the percentages, your own experience likely supports this assertion. If we accept this to be true in principle, the potential for failure underscores the value of the ideas and concepts put forth in the readings contained in this text.

On the surface, we might believe that most or all organizations recognize the significance of people and their development to the success of organizational goals. How many times, for example, have you heard this pronouncement by an executive—"people are our most important asset"? Yet, often in real life, attention is paid to everything but people—capital requirements, cost controls, materials resources, technology or market demands. The gap between policy and practice is apparent, especially to those working down in the organization. Good intentions often end up as nothing more substantial than lip service with cynicism as a likely by-product.

The workplace is one of the most conservative bastions in

America, resisting the changes brought by wave after wave of individualism that have affected so many other aspects of our life. One indicator is the failure to recognize the diminishing impact of the "carrot and stick" approach to incentives for work. However, this oversight alone does not account for the discontent that marks today's work force.

Employee discontent takes several forms. Perhaps the most prevalent and insidious symptom is the passive resistance exhibited by increasing numbers of employees. It's reflected in excessive absenteeism, lateness and slowed productivity. The United States' productivity rate now lags behind most industrialized countries. This translates into increased costs and lowered profits. Another symptom is the growing strength of white-collar unionism. Employees who formerly relied on management to represent their best interests are turning more and more to unions to do so. It's a message we cannot afford to deny or ignore. Experience has shown how innovation and adaptation may be constrained with the advent of third-party representation.

What's behind these and other measures of discontent? I propose that we must re-examine our assumptions about the values and expectations of those who work in organizations like our own. If our response as managers is to be on target, we must continue to learn more about the needs and desires of our employees.

CHANGING VALUES AND EXPECTATIONS

One of the articles earlier in this book looks at the issue "what employees really want from their jobs." The survey cited revealed a significant discrepancy between what employees said they wanted and what their managers thought they wanted. It was conducted well over ten years ago. Could such a gap exist today? Could we be operating on the basis of outmoded assumptions about what people want?

A recent study (1978) evaluated current job values and contrasted them with those that have been in place. The results warrant our careful review, for they may well determine how effective future efforts are in responding to the dynamics of the workplace. The following diagram vividly portrays the significant changes that were revealed in the latest survey:

121

PAST VALUES	PRESENT VALUES
Employees tolerated many negative features of work to earn a decent living and gain a measure of economic security for the family.	Work force is much less willing to put up with what they consider unreasonable organizational demands or conditions.
Work predominated one's activities. Leisure time was limited and had to be fitted around work schedules.	Pursuit of leisure is becoming more important compared to work and family.
Most people defined their identity through their work role, suppressing most conflicting personal desires.	Refusal to subordinate personalities to the work role; preoccupation with self and personal needs.
Significant loyalty and attachment to the organization.	Premium on job mobility; increased loyalty to one's profession or trade.
Incentive system comprised mainly of money and rewards; the "carrot and stick" approach.	Look beyond money; seeking self-actualization, including personal growth and more control over the job setting itself.
A woman's place was in the home—if the family could afford it.	A paid job has become the symbol of independence and self-worth for many women. The number of women in the job force has doubled since 1956.

This same survey revealed that most people enter a job willing to work hard and be productive. But if the job fails to give them the incentives they seek, they then lose interest—or leave.

Some of us may find these results unsettling, just more evidence of a society gone "soft." We may even choose to reject them. They may, however, provide clues to enable us to respond more appropriately. If people are indeed our most important asset and we are not satisfied with our present results, there are options available to us. Organizations and individual managers have discovered practical, effective ways of dealing with the realities that confront us.

MANAGEMENT'S RESPONSE

The 1980's will see the extension of already existing trends, namely:

- Greater complexity in business; rapid changes and accompanying crises.

122

- More governmental impact on our organizations and how we manage.
- Decreasing job security as the era of unrestricted growth nears an end.
- An increasing awareness that the individual matters.

In the face of these conditions and the other issues raised throughout this book about why people work (and don't work), organizations must energetically seek more productive responses.

The following is a description of just two systems or techniques that show promise in helping us make the workplace a desirable and challenging setting. These approaches have one thing in common that should appeal to the pragmatic manager of today and the future—*they work*. They also take into account the new value system cited previously.

QUALITY CONTROL CIRCLES

In 1977, over 12 million vehicles were recalled in the United States to check for potential defects. A major tire manufacturer is spending millions of dollars to recall and replace a purportedly defective tire. These and other tales vividly convey the costs and loss of public confidence due to quality problems. A new approach to quality improvement, originated in Japan, has begun to gain favor in the United States. It's called Quality Control Circles.

A Quality Control Circle consists of a small group of employees (8-10) doing similar work that meets regularly to identify, analyze and solve product quality problems. Before beginning their work, each employee is trained in a participative problem solving system. This system helps him focus on problems arising from materials, methods, manpower and machines. Employees learn how to investigate, chart and prioritize the identified problems—then recommend solutions to management.

Secondly, supervisors receive training on how to organize and maintain Quality Control (QC) Circles. In this way, the first-line manager becomes an integral and important component. His or her job is enriched in the process.

Participants in QC Circles are volunteers—no one is forced to join. The QC Circle is based on the premise that production employees are indeed creative and, given the proper environment and tools, they will think and act in a manner constructive to the firm. By asking the individual to be creative and to improve his/her job by solving work-related problems, the QC Circle cuts to the heart of motivation. The Circle does not motivate per se, but provides the supportive environment needed for the individual to be motivated.

Where installed, worker response has been heavily in favor of QC Circles. The acceptance level of participants has ranged from 80% to 95%. A significant by-product is the improved communications between employees and management. The existence of a union has not been a deterrent either. Of course, the local union should be apprised of the methods and goals of QC Circles. In a number of locations, union stewards have become members of the Circle.

QC Circles help tap the creativity and desire of employees to make a meaningful contribution to their work. Frederick Herzberg, the noted motivational theorist, states that a good job has these elements—opportunities for learning, direct communications, feedback and personal accountability. QC Circles incorporate all of these ingredients.

But what benefits accrue to the organization? Here are several examples derived from companies now employing QC Circles:

- Elimination of work delays caused by tool calibration procedures. New calibration procedures were established. Savings: *$86,000.*

- Reduction in plastic part fabrication. A technique was developed by the Circle to reduce the molding process from five steps to two. The revised assembly was stronger, lighter and has increased reliability. Estimated Savings: *$160,000.*

- Elimination of failures resulting from mating flat ribbon cable to cylindrical connector. A metal guide was designed and new techniques devised. Savings: *$11,500.*

- Clerical employees effected changes that reduced the error rate by 50% and no packages were lost or misrouted. First Year Savings: *$62,400.*

One of the chief attractions to management is that there is no need to add staff to achieve results like these. In addition, the ratio of savings to costs averages six-to-one. Productivity increases typically run from 10% to 20% annually. And, of course, quality rates show improvement too.

QC Circles have been most often initiated in manufacturing units. However, successful projects have been created in clerical, engineering, materials control and other service areas.

Consultants in QC Circles are available to help an organization implement the concept. Professionally designed training materials are provided at a relatively modest cost.

A properly planned and implemented QC Circles program, with full management backing, can boost productivity and lower product defects. At the same time, it inspires more effective teamwork and promotes job involvement and employee motivation.

PERFORMANCE IMPROVEMENT

A familiar lament from many managers, often with good cause, concerns the performance level of their employees—output is down, scrap up, procedures not followed—a prescription for crisis or "fire fighting."

For the past ten years a number of top U.S. corporations have been experimenting with a system of management based on behavior modification concepts popularized by Harvard psychologist, B. F. Skinner. Not all experiments have been successful but the overall results have been promising, so much so that, Ford Motor Company, Proctor & Gamble, IBM and Emery Air Freight and others have implemented the system in major units of their organizations.

The premise is relatively simple in principle; give employees frequent, relatively immediate feedback on their performance and positive reinforcement (some form of reward) for satisfactory performance and results tend to improve.

In essence, when employees know better how they are doing and get something they like or want for a certain specified level of performance, performance improves and can be maintained. The reward that is contingent upon good performance in a given work environment acts as a motivator for future performance. The manager, by controlling the environment, task assignments and consequences of job performance in a way that makes them positive for his subordinates, can contribute substantially toward higher productivity.

Our present reward system in industry is often out of "synch." Rewards don't relate to individual performance; or they are based on seniority; or the interval between performance and reward is so great as to diminish its impact . . . or there is no reward at all.

Performance improvement, based on positive reinforcement, addresses the issue of incentives for the new breed of worker and the value system that puts a premium on self-development or "self-actualization," to use Maslow's term.

There are four basic essential steps involved when introducing such a system into an organization.

1. *Performance Analysis or Audit*—identifying the critical behaviors affecting performance in the job. Causes of poor performance are identified. Present level of performance is established.

2. *Establish Feedback Systems*—goals are quantified so performance can be measured accurately and fed back to employees on a set schedule. Workers often are involved in keeping records so they produce their own performance feedback.

3. *Positive Reinforcement Program*—an action plan is developed by the manager so that good performance is rewarded as frequently as needed to sustain desired performance levels. Reinforcers are selected. Rewards may take the form of money but more often entail praise, special privileges and/or recognition.

4. *Implementation*—step by step introduction in selected work unit(s), usually on a pilot basis.

To successfully implement a Performance Improvement System demands management commitment, training of managers in using the concepts properly and an ongoing evaluation of results. Companies often utilize the services of an outside consultant who serves as Project Manager for the launch and follow-up assessment. As with QC Circles, this system can operate in union and non-union environments. And there are documented, often impressive, results obtained. For example:

- a telephone company increased attendance performance by 50%;
- productivity increased 33% in a large paper manufacturer;
- a metropolitan city saved over $1.5 million and reduced citizen complaints in one service department;
- turnaround time on machine repairs reduced by ⅓ for an electronics firm.

The typical return on investment to costs ratio is 4:1, but this depends upon the organization's goals and the areas chosen for implementation. In any event, the results to date warrant the attention of all managers who have a stake in enhancing profits, productivity and employee satisfaction.

SUMMARY

Neither QC Circles nor Performance Improvement (positive reinforcement) systems are offered as a panacea. We have all had our fill of "easy solutions." They do suggest that there *are* innovative, rather exciting ways for managers to build the organizational conditions that engender positive worker behavior.

It is *not* a time for lament or disenchantment or resistance to change. It is a time for experimentation, of risking, of setting out in new directions. To quote John Gardner, "The society (or organization) capable of continuous renewal not only feels at home with the future, it accepts, even welcomes, the idea that the future may bring change." The challenge is clear and compelling. The next decade is going to test all managers as no period in our history has since the Industrial Revolution. Will you be a *participant* or a *bystander* in the renaissance that is bound to sweep through business and industry?

REFERENCES

Burrow, Martha. Developing Women Managers. *AMA Survey Report,* Sept. 1978, p. 2.

GARDNER, JOHN. *Self-Renewal: The Individual and the Innovative Society.* New York: Harper and Rowe, 1963.

HAMMER, W. CLAY and ELLEN, P. Behavior Modification on the Bottom Line. *Organizational Dynamics*, February 1976, pp. 3-21.

LEVINSON, HARRY. *Psychological Man.* Cambridge, Mass.: The Levinson Institute, 1976.

New Tool: Reinforcement for Good Work. *Business Week*, December 18, 1971, pp. 70-71.

RENWICK, PATRICIA A. and LAWLER, EDWARD E. What You Really Want from Your Job. *Psychology Today*, Vol. 2, No. 12, May 1978, pp. 53-65.

ROSOW, JEROME. Work Trends in the '80's: Obstacles and Opportunities. *Training*, October 1978, pp. 62-63.

WEINTRAUB, RONALD. Why Even Presidents and Vice Presidents Need Training and Development. *Training*, October 1978, pp. 47-48.

YANKELOVICH, DANIEL. The New Psychological Contracts at Work. *Psychology Today*, Vol. 2, No. 12, May 1978, pp. 46-50.

DATE DUE

JA 3 '89			
DE 20 '93			
GAYLORD			PRINTED IN U.S.A.